Maids, Wives, Widows

This book is dedicated with much love to my Nanna, Annie (b. 1924), matriarch extraordinaire.

Maids, Wives, Widows

Exploring Early Modern Women's Lives 1540–1740

Sara Read

PEN & SWORD
HISTORY

First published in Great Britain in 2015 by
Pen & Sword History
an imprint of
Pen & Sword Books Ltd
47 Church Street
Barnsley
South Yorkshire
S70 2AS

ISBN 978 1 47382 340 2

A CIP catalogue record for this book is available from the British
Library

Typeset in Ehrhardt by
Mac Style Ltd, Bridlington, East Yorkshire
Printed and bound in the UK by CPI Group (UK) Ltd,
Croydon, CRO 4YY

Pen & Sword Books Ltd incorporates the imprints of Pen & Sword
Archaeology, Atlas, Aviation, Battleground, Discovery, Family
History, History, Maritime, Military, Naval, Politics, Railways, Select,
Transport, True Crime, and Fiction, Frontline Books, Leo Cooper,
Praetorian Press, Seaforth Publishing and Wharncliffe.

For a complete list of Pen & Sword titles please contact
PEN & SWORD BOOKS LIMITED
47 Church Street, Barnsley, South Yorkshire, S70 2AS, England
E-mail: enquiries@pen-and-sword.co.uk
Website: www.pen-and-sword.co.uk

Contents

List of Illustrations

A page from Lady Ann Fanshawe's 'Recipe Book, containing Medical, Culinary and other Recipes, compiled from 1651.' (Wellcome Library, London)

Adriaen van Ostade, 'A Woman Breast-feeding her Child Amongst her Family' (1641). (Wellcome Library, London)

Etching of three pregnant women, taken from a German medical text (1546). (Wellcome Library, London)

'A dissection of the womb' from Jane Sharp's *The Complete Midwives Companion* (1724). (Wellcome Library, London)

An Italian woman named Dorothy who reputedly had twenty children at to births. From Ambroise Paré, *The Works of that Famous Surgeon Amboise Parey* (1678). (Wellcome Library, London)

Figures of babies in the womb. From Eucharius Rösslin, *The Birth of Mankind* (1604). (Wellcome Library, London)

'A woman seated on a obstetrical chair giving birth aided by a midwife who works beneath her skirts.' From Eucharius Rösslin, *Rosengarten* (1513). (Wellcome Library, London)

Birthing stool and babies in the womb, from another edition of Eucharius Rösslin, *The Birth of Mankind* (1565). (Wellcome Library, London)

'Mr Giffard's extractor forceps as improved by Mr Freke.' From William Giffard's *Cases in Midwifry* (1734). (Wellcome Library, London)

'A woman giving birth aided by a surgeon who fumbles beneath a sheet to save the lady from embarrassment' (1711). (Wellcome Library, London)

'A seated woman giving birth aided by a midwife and two other attendants, in the background two men are looking at the stars and plotting a horoscope' (1583). (Wellcome Library, London)

Scene after the birth of a child. From Jakob Rüf, *De Conceptu et Generatione Hominis* (1580). (Wellcome Library, London)

The frontispiece to Jane Sharp's *The Complete Midwives Companion* (1724). (Wellcome Library, London)

Bathing a baby (1546). (Wellcome Library, London)

Child with feeding bottle (1546). (Wellcome Library, London)

Child in a baby walker/playpen (1577). (Wellcome Library, London)

Child potty training (1577). (Wellcome Library, London)

Francesco Cozza, 'Pero breastfeeding her father Cimon to assuage his hunger,' Seventeenth Century. (Wellcome Library, London)

'Elizabeth Hopkins of Oxford, showing a breast with cancer which was removed by Sir William Read. Engraving by M. Burghers, ca. 1700.' (Wellcome Library, London)

Ann Clarke, aged 53, suffering from breast cancer. (Wellcome Library, London)

'Caricature of female barber-surgeons bloodletting from a patient's foot' (1695). (Wellcome Library, London)

'A clyster [an enema] in use. Oil painting by a French painter, ca. 1700.' (Wellcome Library, London)

A woman being let blood from her ankle (1623). (Wellcome Library, London)

'The doctor's dispensary and the apothecary's shop in the 17th century.' From Nicolas Culpeper's translation of *The Expert Doctors Dispensatory* (1657). (Wellcome Library, London)

'Title page of 'News from the Dead,' a book of poetry about Anne Greene who was executed at Oxford and afterwards revived' by Richard Watkins (1651). (Wellcome Library, London)

'Mary Tofts [or Toft], a woman who pretended that she had given birth to rabbits. Coloured stipple engraving by Maddocks (1819).' (Wellcome Library, London)

John and Mary Champian, depicted after Mary murdered their son. Credit: The Lewis Walpole Library, Yale University

'Sarah Malcolm sitting in prison with her hands resting on a table. Engraving by T. Cook after W. Hogarth' (1802). (Wellcome Library, London)

The ruins of Brampton Bryan Castle, Herefordshire which was the home of the Harley family. (Pete Read)

Brampton Bryan Castle: the upper storey is thought to have been Brilliana, Lady Harley's chamber. (Pete Read)

Aston Hall, Birmingham, built by Sir Thomas Holte between 1618 and 1635. (Pete Read)

Blakesley Hall, Yardley, Birmingham dates from 1590, and was built by Richard Smalbroke of one of the rising merchant class families. (Pete Read)

Selly Manor, Bourneville, Birmingham, showing the overhanging eaves typical of houses from this time. (Pete Read)

A priest hole at Selly Manor. (Pete Read)

Little Moreton Hall, Congleton, Cheshire. (Pete Read)

Acknowledgements

This book has been a pleasure to write and I'd like to thank Pen & Sword for their enthusiastic and swift response to my proposal. I am grateful for the support of my colleagues in the School of Arts, English and Drama, at Loughborough University, especially those in the Early Modern Research Group.

I'd like to thank Deirdre O'Byrne for her enthusiasm towards this project, Katie Aske for putting me right about the true meaning of 'puppywater' (see Chapter 6), and Claire Bowditch for explaining that Aphra was in fact a reasonably common Christian name in seventeenth century Kent (see Introduction). My grateful thanks go to my former officemate and close friend Rachel Adcock for her superb clothing illustration and for reviewing my chapters on religion.

I'd like to thank Jen Evans for her support and for the work she puts into her blog *earlymodernmedicine.com*, which I not only enjoy co-editing but from which I also learn so much.

I owe a great deal to the Wellcome Trust for their decision to make their library of digital images freely available, and have sourced many of the illustrations here from this wonderful collection.

I want to acknowledge too, the lively discussion that has grown up on Twitter, where scholars interested in any aspect of historical research pool information using the #twitterstorians and #medhist hashtags. These hashtags link to a myriad of blog posts and informative discussions. I'm on Twitter on @*floweringbodies* and always happy to hear from others with shared interests.

The chapter on childbirth is an expanded version of an article which appeared in *Discover Your Ancestors*, volume 3, in February 2014 and I am grateful to the editor for permission to include it here.

My thanks go to Jen Newby and Eloise Hansen at Pen & Sword for making the publication process so smooth and pleasant.

And final thanks, as ever, go to my whole family for their continued support.

Dr Sara Read, 2014

A Note on Original Texts

All early modern quotations have been modernised to make the sense accessible while retaining the original meaning. The legal calendar started on March 25 in the seventeenth century, even though people celebrated the New Year on 1 January, as we do. This means though, that any dates before 25 March fell within what we would perceive as the previous year. Any dates have therefore been regularised to match the modern calendar.

The first time an individual is referred to, their dates of birth and death (where known) are given; these also appear in the index. Details of all the texts quoted or from which information is taken, are listed in the Bibliography.

Introduction

Arise early
Serve God devoutly
Then to thy work busily
To thy meat joyfully
To thy bed merrily
And though thou fare poorly
And thy lodging homely
Yet thank God highly.

(Bartholomew Dowe,
Dairy Book for Housewives, 1588)

So Katharine Dowe advised, according to her son Bartholomew in his *Dairy Book for Housewives* (1588). Katharine worked as a dairy farmer and her words sum up many aspects of the lives of early modern women. Being devout, working hard, eating well were attributes that most conduct books of the day recommended. They also match the best medical opinion of early modern times, which saw a cheerful disposition, good food, hard work and sufficient rest as a model for good health. All of these areas of women's lives will be demonstrated in the following chapters.

The early modern era is generally taken to be the time immediately after the medieval period up until the late eighteenth century, although this book focuses on the seventeenth century in particular. The title of this book, *Maids, Wives, Widows*, is taken from the legal classification of women in early modern times. This triad was widely used by men and women to indicate the status of an individual woman. While the legal definition of women according to their marital status is a useful starting point, I hope this book will leave readers with a sense of how varied, rich, joyous, and sociable early modern women's lives were, not to mention just how busy or difficult they could be. There is not just one type of early modern woman, whether maid, wife or widow, and this book will give varied examples of women's different personalities and different economic circumstances.

Maids, Wives, Widows also aims to give a real sense of how an early modern woman filled her days, covering topics such as: what she might have eaten; how she kept well; what she wore; who she socialised with; what she read; what sort of paid work was available to her; how and when she married. The details of daily life are also explored, for instance how women coped with periods, with breastfeeding, and with childbirth on top of everything else. The following chapters are intended to provide a tour through many facets of women's everyday lives in England between 1540 and 1740.

During this period a virgin or unmarried woman of any age, from a baby to an elderly unmarried woman, was known as a maid, while 'wife' or 'widow' similarly classified the remainder in terms of their marital status. Although, in some circumstances, a single woman could be defined as a *femme sole* and have legal rights over her own affairs, generally speaking, in the first two categories women were under the legal control of their father or husband respectively. A married woman took on the status of a *femme covert*, which meant that she no longer had a legal identity but was subsumed into that of her husband.

Widowhood, by contrast, was a state in which a woman might have some control over her own life, probably for the first time. For a start she now became the legal owner of her property. A widow was commonly afforded a jointure, or settlement, in her husband's will, which allowed her a third of his estate, at least until she remarried, hence the phrase 'a widow's thirds.' For titled widows the term dowager was normally added before their name to show their husband was dead, but ordinary women were often referred to as 'widow' in place of 'mistress' (a term which applied equally to single and married women). The Somerset apothecary John Westover's notebook regularly entitles women in this way; for instance on 19 March 1686 he noted that 'Widow Langcassel of Blackford' sought treatment for a sore mouth.

As a wife, until the Married Women's Property Act of 1870, anything a woman brought to the marriage, even her eventual children and her own body were the legal property of her husband. A telling but typical example of the way that women were subsumed into their husband's identity is seen in a diary comment made by Mary Woodforde (d. 1730) on the marriage of her step-daughter Alice. On 18 July 1689, Mary described how Alice had married Alexander Dalgress, but in the next entry on 22 July Mary records, 'Mr Dalgress had his wife home to his parsonage.' Women themselves were conscious of this change in their identity, which went beyond a legal definition, and they often expressed it in terms similar to Yorkshire gentlewoman, Alice Thornton (1626–1707), who recounted in her autobiography that, on marriage, she had left her 'youth and virgin estate' to enter into her 'new condition' as a wife.

Despite the fact that wives held the legal status of non-persons and were subject to the rule of their husbands, there were many happy and successful matches, in which both parties showed mutual trust and respect. John Lilburne, who married around 1640 and ran a brewery with his new wife Elizabeth Dewell, wrote to a friend that the first few months of marriage were 'commonly a time of dotage,' suggesting that couples were so wrapped up in one another that they temporarily lost their minds.

On 16 May 1594, Lady Maria Touchet (c.1578–1611), the daughter of Lord Audley, secretly married Thomas Thynne, heir to Longleat, much to his family's dismay, since their fathers were adversaries. The scandal this caused has been given as one reason why William Shakespeare revived the old love story of star-crossed lovers Romeo and Juliet into a play for the Globe Theatre shortly afterwards. In a letter to her husband, written some years later, Maria declared that she regarded him 'many thousand times more than these 1 000 000 000 000 000 000 000 000 00 for thy kind wanton letters,' showing the love and sexual attraction the pair still enjoyed.

A hundred years later, the letters of Elizabeth, Lady Bristol (1676–1741) to her husband, John Hervey, first earl of Bristol, similarly reveal deep affection. Elizabeth often lamented the time Hervey spent away at Court, where he was a favourite of Queen Anne (1665–1714), and even went so far as to say that she found the pain of his absence greater than any other bodily pain, except labour. Since Lady Bristol had 17 children between 1698 and 1716, she had a very good idea of what labour pains felt like.

There are records of unhappy marriages, of course, such as that of Frances Carr, Countess of Somerset (1592–1632) whose first marriage to Robert Devereux, third earl of Essex, was eventually annulled in 1613 for non-consummation, due to their mutual antipathy. In the annulment hearing Devereux admitted impotence, but said he had no such difficulties with other women.

Surviving letters show early modern marriages to have had their ups and downs, then as now. The early seventeenth century letters of the Knyvetts are a good example of this. Sir Thomas Knyvett's letters to his wife allow us to infer her frustration at having to rely on him to source goods and services in London, while she was stuck in the Norfolk countryside and he was in Parliament. In one letter from late 1623, Thomas remarked on his disappointment that Katherine (d. 1646) was so cross with him that she had neglected to give him news of their children, but generally his letters are full of expressions of love and court gossip.

As the brief examples discussed already show, the first names of the early modern women featured in this book are mostly ones that we are still familiar with. Whilst it is now common to have two forenames, William Camden observed that it was most unusual for people to be given more than one Christian name in early modern times. His book, *Remaines of a Greater Work Concerning Britain* (1605), gives a list of the most frequently used women's names at the time: Agnes, Alice, Anna, Bridget, Catherine (pronounced with a hard 't'), Diana, Dorothy, Elizabeth and the derivatives of it, Grace, Jane, Judith, Joyce, Laura, Margaret, Marie (Mary), Penelope, Phyllis, Rachel, Rebecca, Rose, Sarah, Susan, Sophia, Tabitha, Ursula and Winifred. Most of these names are still in use now, although some move in and out of fashion through the decades.

Naming trends were just the same in the early modern period. For example, Camden noted that Jane was a relatively new name, which 'the better and nicer sort' of people have taken to using instead of Joan, which despite being a well-known medieval royal name, was by this time considered a bit down-market. Camden wrote that this change was as recent as Henry VIII's reign.

There were also women's names derived from male names, such as Frances, Phillipa, Joanna (John), Tamesin (or Thomasin, from Thomas). Others are more unusual and include Adrian, Dennis, and Douglas, which were often taken from family surnames. For instance, Lady Douglas Sheffield (1542–1608) had an acknowledged illegitimate child with Elizabeth I's favourite Robert Dudley, Earl of Leicester. The name Avice (one example is Avisa Allen

(1560–1597), a mistress of Elizabeth I's astronomer Simon Forman), was a usual Christian name, which derives from the same root as the boy's name Lewis. The playwright Aphra Behn's (1640–1689) Christian name was quite a common one in Kent when she was born, albeit with various spellings.

Some of the elite women mentioned in this book have more exotic names, however. For example, Brilliana, Lady Harley (1598–1643), who was named after Brielle in the Netherlands, where she was born, and Lady Dionys Fitzherbert (1580–1641), who was named after the Greek god of fertility, Dionysus.

Names could indicate a woman's social position and religious persuasion, and while there was no direct equivalent of the modern British class system at this time, society was heavily ordered around social rank. This followed a belief that it was natural that some were born to rule and others to serve. There was a burgeoning middle class, known as the 'middling sort,' as the merchant classes made money from trading. Often wealthy merchants' families and impoverished aristocratic families looked to broker marriage deals, ennobling one side whilst financing the other. This book examines the lives of women of all ranks.

A woman's rank in society had a direct bearing on the shape of her life and day-to-day activities. Elite women had fewer material concerns than poorer women, but these were traded for a lack of freedom. Both Margaret Cavendish, Duchess of Newcastle (1623–1673), and Lady Hester Pulter (1605–1678) railed against being shut up in their 'country granges,' with Cavendish likening elite women to caged birds shut away in their often magnificent homes. They often envied the freedom ordinary women had to call on their friends and pass the time of day.

Lady Elizabeth Delaval (1649–1717) also lamented that as a wife and role model for servants in her household she would have to act more soberly, as the fun and laughter of a maid were not considered appropriate conduct in a high-ranking wife. These women were responsible for the welfare of large numbers of people, while running homes which resembled small businesses with large budgets to manage. Elite women were normally married in their teens, in arranged political or financially convenient matches. They might have large numbers of children, at a rate of one child every 18 months until the menopause, which women then expected in their late forties.

Often, high-ranking women were forbidden, or at least discouraged, from breastfeeding their babies themselves and they did not usually bring up their own children. It was normal in aristocratic circles for boys aged from seven to be sent to other households, preferably of people higher up the social scale still, for their education. Girls stayed at home longer, but might go into service at the court or in the households of their superiors when they became teenagers. Women lower down the social ranks would have had more say in who they married, and wed much later, on average in their mid-twenties. They would be more likely to have raised their own children, but their concerns were focussed on the practical aspects of making enough money to bring up these children to adulthood. Differences and similarities within the lives of women of different ranks will be discussed within each chapter.

A relationship with God was at the heart of women's lives in this period. As every event was deemed to be due to God's will, prayers were said about most decisions, such as when Mary Woodforde and her husband deliberated taking their son out of school and sending him instead to Cambridge University. At this time women were thought to be weaker than men in both soul and body, and therefore more susceptible to attacks on their spiritual as well as bodily health. These beliefs stem from the Biblical precedent of Eve, who succumbed to the Devil's temptations in the Garden of Eden, dooming her female descendants with the punishment of painful childbirth.

Both men and women looked for signs that they were in favour with God and interpreted life events as direct spiritual messages. A miscarriage, for example, was often taken as a sign of God's displeasure over a lack of piety, or a reminder that life and death were subject to God's ordinance and pleasure. In a letter to her mother, Lady Joan Barrington (c.1558–1641), written in 1629, Lady Elizabeth Masham (d. by 1656) wrote that illness could serve as a way of reminding a woman that her earthly suffering would end when she was admitted to heaven:

all the distempers of our bodies, which must need be many while we live here [on earth], *may be a* [...] *means of the curing the great distemper of our souls, and may make us long for that home where all sorrows have an end and we shall triumph in joy and glory forever more.*

This religious concern was why Mary Woodforde wrote in 1685, when she had some blood let from her arm upon doctor's orders, that she believed 'it may help my body as to make it more serviceable to my soul.' This book, therefore, has many instances of the central position religion occupied in people's daily lives.

Early modern society differed greatly from our own in the understanding of bodies as well as souls. The human body was thought to function based on a series of bodily fluids, known as humours, which needed to remain in balance to maintain health. This ancient system had been inherited from the Classical Greek teachings of Hippocrates (460 BCE–approx 370 BCE), often called the father of modern medicine. Humoral medicine was then further refined and systematised by the Roman physician and writer Claudius Galen (129–c.216 CE).

The four main liquids or humours in the body were believed to be connected to the four elements of the earth: blood was related to air and spring; yellow bile (choler) to fire and summer; black bile (melancholy) to the earth and autumn; and phlegm to water and winter. Personality was also seen as linked to your humoral make-up, so an irritable person would be assumed to produce too much yellow bile. Similarly, the symptoms of what we would think of as depression were linked to having too much black bile, or melancholy, and steps would have been taken to rebalance the humours of someone diagnosed as melancholic. There was also a gender bias, with women's bodies seen as naturally colder and wetter than the hot and dry male.

The way that early modern physicians believed a female body was constructed often followed an idea set out by Galen, who argued that women's reproductive organs were essentially the same as men's but that women's were positioned internally for warmth, as women's bodies were colder than men's. So then, the vagina was like a penis and the womb like the scrotum and so on. This became known as the 'one-sex' model, but even when it was the most popular biological explanation available, no-one thought that men and women's bodies worked in the same way.

One of the key ways in which the female body was understood was through the effect that her womb had on it. One famous, often reprinted, quotation was from a letter written to Hippocrates in ancient times. A seventeenth century translation of the letter gave it as, 'the womb is the cause of six hundred miseries and innumerable calamities.' One of these calamities was even believed to be breast cancer, which was thought to be caused by a humoral imbalance linked to irregular or stopped periods. The womb and the breasts were thought to be linked by a 'mamilliary vein' (which in fact does not exist), which sent menstrual blood up to the breast, for it to be turned into milk after a birth. If the woman was not lactating or having periods, the assumption was that her blood could be sent up through this system, corrupting the body and potentially causing cancer.

This theory is important in building a sense of how early modern women thought of themselves and in understanding the role their reproductive bodies had on their lives. People of all ranks 'knew' the trouble the womb could cause women, with treatments for things like fits of the mother (womb) being recorded in apothecary records on a regular basis. Because of the centrality of the womb to the health of early modern women this book explores early modern attitudes to menstruation, childbirth, and breastfeeding in dedicated chapters.

A proverb from the early seventeenth century claimed, 'England is the paradise of women, the purgatory of men, and the hell of horses.' The reasoning behind this saying was that women had more freedom than their continental neighbours to go out and about in the day time, to visit friends and neighbours, and to shop without a male escort. However, not everyone thought this apparent freedom was a good thing. In their conduct guidebook, *A Godly Form of Household Management* (1598), Robert Dod and John Cleaver denounced women who went visiting: 'The woman that gads from house to house to prate [*gossip*] confounds herself, her husband and her family.' In the following chapters, *Maids, Wives, Widows* gives some serious but also quirky examples of attitudes like these, both of and towards, women in this era. How far early modern England seems like it was a paradise for women will be left for the reader to judge.

The book is arranged into five sections of related chapters. Section I is concerned with women's work and how the early modern woman filled her days, and so covers everything from the work of the housewife and mother of older children to the paid occupations women had. Section II looks at personal care in terms of what women liked to eat and drink, what they wore and personal hygiene and beauty regimes. Section III examines all aspects of women's reproductive lives, from the menarche to the menopause. Section IV focuses on spirituality and investigates religion and daily life, as well as the part women played in the various non-conformist religions which flourished in the seventeenth century. The final section looks at the position of women in public life: their dealings with the courts, their involvement with politics, and when they wrote for publication.

By better understanding the lives of our ancestors we come to a more complete sense of how we came to be where we are today, and the ways in which women's daily lives have changed over the centuries. We also notice aspects of their lives which are still recognisable to us today. Women earned a living, brought up families and loved, as do most modern women. The material world around them was undoubtedly different but their concerns will seem familiar to many.

Part I

Women's Work

Chapter One

'Goodwives':
Marriage and Housewifery

While for the upper ranks marriage was usually organised by anything other than mutual affection, women lower down the ranks had far more freedom in choosing their husband. The growing upper middle-classes attempted to use their wealth to imitate the aristocracy and arrange advantageous marriages between their children and those who lacked ready money but possessed a title, thus ennobling their family. The majority of young people though, met at work, at the market, in church and in the general course of life. For the average couple, marriage didn't take place until their mid-twenties, once they had finished apprenticeships and established themselves and were in a position to live as a married couple.

Couples usually became betrothed or engaged before marriage; a promise to marry was taken much more seriously than an engagement is today. Indeed, if a previous betrothal was discovered, it was a legitimate legal impediment to marrying someone else. One of the tactics Thomas Cromwell unsuccessfully tried to use to invalidate Henry VIII's marriage to Lady Anne Boleyn (1501–1536) was to smoke out evidence of a pre-contract between Anne and Henry Percy, Earl of Northumberland.

A betrothal, referred to as 'handfasting,' was a ceremony where couples 'plighted their faith or troth' or promised to marry one another in the future. There did not need to be any witnesses to handfasting for it to be lawful, nor was any subsequent marriage required. Until the 1753 Marriage Act, an act designed to end clandestine marriages, such as Maria Thynne's (see Introduction), a marriage ceremony could be as simple as two people declaring to one another that they took each other to be husband and wife in the present tense. Obviously, it was better to have witnesses, for the marriage to be proven to have taken place and for there to be no question of the couple's children's legitimacy, so most people would make their vows in front of a priest and their families. Also, unofficial marriages were not recognised by the Church, and couples so married risked excommunication.

Another advantage of a marriage in church was that, long after all the witnesses had died or moved away, there would still be a record by the church register to prove the wedding had taken place. However, the new 'Puritan' forms of Protestantism, which grew out of the Reformation in the sixteenth century, saw church weddings as unbiblical and opted for quiet weddings at home, in which they even rejected the exchanging of rings.

Indeed, for a brief time during the Interregnum (1649–1660) when England was a commonwealth, following an Act of Parliament (1653) marriage became a purely civil ceremony, with the Church no longer involved. However, the Restoration of the monarchy in 1660 reset the legislative clock to the day of Charles I's death and all laws passed by Parliament during the Interregnum were voided.

Because of the seriousness of handfasting, in the eyes of the community, the Church and the law, couples would often begin to sleep together after they were betrothed, not bothering with the marriage ceremony until a baby was on the way, which had the advantage of bringing known fertility to the match. This accounts for the fact that, while there were very few illegitimate births, up to 30 per cent of brides were expecting when they wed. Famously, 18-year-old William Shakespeare, a minor, was married by special licence in November 1582 to 26-year-old Anne Hathaway, who was around three months pregnant.

To marry in church usually required the banns (or a notice of the forthcoming marriage) to be read on three consecutive Sundays and this would have avoided the costly special licence. However, William and Anne would have wanted the marriage to be legitimised by the Church for the sake of their unborn child, and the licence saved time. Having the banns read would also have delayed their marriage beyond the three weeks, as Advent was then approaching, a period when, in common with most important Church festivals, marriages were not supposed to be celebrated. As time went on the pregnancy would become more obvious, and they evidently wished to avoid this.

Upon marriage, women of the middle and lower ranks were often known by the title 'Goody,' short for 'goodwife' or dame, in the way we use 'Mrs.' 'Mrs' is the short form of 'mistress,' then used to address all women below the aristocracy, so it did not give any indication of a woman's marital status in the way that Goody does. Indeed, women were entitled to be addressed as 'mistress' or 'Mrs' at all stages of life. The case notes of John Hall the Stratford-on-Avon doctor, and Shakespeare's son-in-law, include numerous examples of this. For example, he treated unmarried 17-year-old gentlewoman 'Mrs Mary Murden' in 1617, for problems with her periods.

The Role of the English Housewife

Gervase Markham published a book describing the role of the English housewife in 1625. It had been reprinted at least five times by 1648. Markham wrote that the first duty of a housewife was to be godly and to learn from her husband. She was to act as a role model for the family through her example of piety: the key duty of a housewife was the moral welfare of the family, which at that time was taken to include anyone who lived in the household, including servants.

Most people, apart from the poorest, would employ a maid at least, if not more staff. Essex minister Ralph Josselin (1617–1683) hired his family's first maid, Sarah Brown, shortly after his marriage in 1640, on a salary of £1 18 shillings per year. Like the children of the family, the maid and other servants might sleep on a 'truckle' bed, a bed which could be stowed away under the main bed in the daytime, in their master's bedroom, or in the kitchen on a bench or 'shelf.' From this practice, since maids were single women, the saying being 'left on the shelf' is said to have have derived. Private diaries such as Josselin's refer to the constant comings and goings of domestic maids. Josselin recorded how one maid, Joan, had to return home as her mother was suffering from 'black urine.'

Jane Josselin was around 24 at this time and, according to her husband, was not yet an accomplished housewife. He lamented in April 1646 that Jane 'fails somewhat in her household diligence,' and he seemed to panic whenever they were left without a maid for whatever reason, praying for one to be quickly sent to them. In December that same year a maid called Margaret left them and a family friend, Mrs Mary, helped the Josselins engage a new maid, Elizabeth, because she knew what 'grief it would be to us to be destitute but a few days.'

'Kitchen Physic': Medical Remedies and Herbal Cures

Markham then stated that it was a housewife's job to keep the household healthy. Many other books made the same point too. In 1685 the title of Thomas Tryon's book, *The Good Housewife made a Doctor*, demonstrates this sentiment. Tryon believed that food was the cure and cause of most diseases and conditions. He firmly believed that poor preparation of food often caused illness and so his treatise is ordered around recipes and practical information, such as how to stop butter from going sour in winter.

Sir Thomas Knyvett referred to so-called 'kitchen physic' in an angry letter to his wife Katherine. He complained that he had heard that when a serious illness affected their daughter Betty, then aged around 23, Katherine had sent for a doctor living 80 miles away, rather than using their regular doctor, the famous physician Sir Thomas Browne. Knyvett told Katherine that Betty had sent him the prescription from the new doctor, who he refers to disparagingly as 'Dick apothecary,' and said that he wouldn't be getting it filled. Instead, since Betty was recovering, he believed that, 'the best and safest course is to cherish her (after so hard a brunt) with good wholesome kitchen physic.'

Knyvett didn't say what Betty's illness was, but Markham took pains to note that housewives couldn't be expected to cure every disease, but should be skilled enough to tend the most common ailments. However, the range of illnesses Markham thought treatable in the home was extensive and even included things from the plague to labour pains and re-growing hair.

While home cures wouldn't help plague victims, it is unsurprising that such cures appeared in books like this one. The disease broke out on a cyclical basis, with epidemics occurring every few years. Most doctors – with the notable exception of Thomas Lodge (1558–1625), who practised during the 1603 outbreak – left London and large conurbations during the plague outbreaks; abandoning their patients to cope as best they could.

During the last major plague outbreak in 1665 a published *Bill of Mortality* stated that 68,596 Londoners died of the plague that year, compared to 625 women who died in childbirth and 1,545 deaths from old age, for example. The highest recorded number of plague deaths in one week was noted between 19-26 September that year, when 7,165 Londoners fell victim to the epidemic. On the 6 July, the government, fearing this epidemic was a punishment from God, had passed a bill declaring the first Wednesday of each month should be kept as a public day of fasting, so that Britons could attempt to atone. Markham described the plague as an inflammation of the blood and suggested that women gave victims cooling drinks such as posset, ale and herbs, while placing a hot brick wrapped in cloth on the soles of their feet.

Often higher-ranking women would provide medical aid to people, both tenants and employees, on their estates, and to do so they relied on their books of physic. In a letter to his mother-in-law Lady Joan Barrington, in 1628, Sir Gilbert Gerard commented that his wife had complained she had not received all her medical books from her mother 'there being an old torn one left behind.' Its tattered appearance suggests the book was well used and Lady Mary, Lady Joan's second youngest daughter clearly relied on it.

Elite women possessed the funds to buy more expensive ingredients and the equipment needed to distil and mix medicines. Ralph and Jane Josselin took their children to the home of one of Ralph's patrons, Lady Hester Honywood (1607–1681), when they were poorly, and she supplied medicines or advice. Lady Grace Mildmay (1552–1620) bequeathed a bundle of medical notes to her daughter, consisting of books and piles of loose papers detailing recipes, case notes, and cures. These notes suggest that Lady Grace was conversant with medical theories at a high level. Lady Margaret Hoby (1571–1633) recorded several episodes in her spiritual diary when she tended to people on her estate. Lady Margaret helped deliver babies and, on one occasion in 1601, even performed surgery, although without success, on a baby born without an opening to his rectum.

Most diseases or conditions a housewife would have attempted to cure were not as serious as the plague, and just a few of the treatments described in Markham's book give a flavour of day-to-day remedies. One cure for lethargy for instance, was to give the sufferer a wine and water mix to drink, then make a loud noise and prevent them from sleeping for any longer than four hours a day. For 'watchfulness' or insomnia, Markham's cure was a paste made from dried saffron, lettuce seeds, and twice as many poppy seeds, mixed in breast milk and applied to the temples.

More obscure recipes include treating the symptoms of epilepsy with a mole of the opposite sex to the sufferer, caught in March or April and dried to a powder in an oven. The power should then be administered in a drink for nine or ten days. Toothache was treated with crushed daisy-roots; bloodshot eyes with egg-white and rose water mixed with leek juice; and mint steeped in white wine might cure a stomach ache. To stop bleeding Markham recommended boiling cinnamon and sugar in claret and drinking the mixture, 'as often as you please.' A condition called 'fatness around the heart' was treated with fennel and honey made into a solid and eaten morning and night to 'consume' the fatness.

Perhaps Markham had personal experience of haemorrhoids, as he described them as 'a troublesome and sore grief' to be treated with dill mixed in sheep suet, or black lead ground to a powder. Finally, constipation known as 'costiveness' was cured with the bark elder tree roots, stamped on, then mixed with old ale and drunk 'in a hearty draft.' The range of illnesses listed in Markham's text is huge as is the variety of cures he suggested, with several options given for many conditions.

Feeding the Early Modern Family

The housewife's next job was feeding her family. Herbs reappear in Gervase Markham's housewifery guide as part of the first, most basic lesson in cookery. What people ate during this period is examined in Chapter Four, and this section is concerned with the processes in the production of food which fell to the housewife. Herbs were used in salads, in the pot, for seasoning, in sauces, and for garnish. It was considered important to pick herbs and vegetables at the right season, which included certain phases of the moon. Garlic and gourds were to be picked at the new moon in February, and cucumbers sown in June at the waning moon.

Markham thought a good cook should not be 'butter-fingered, sweet-toothed, nor faint-hearted' and, given that his advice to know when a pig's head was cooked is that its eyes have dropped out, it is easy to see why he added the last clause. They also should be clean in clothes and person, and use their senses of smell and touch to test their dishes. Housewives needed to know how to source and prepare salads, fricassees, boiled and roasted meats, broths, breads, dairy products, baked meat and pies, oats, as well as fancies and delicacies for parties and celebrations. It was also necessary to be able to preserve vegetables and other produce, malt barley and brew ale. Bread was a staple part of most people's daily diet, so baking was a required skill.

Households would keep a cow for milk, if they could afford to. Markham describes in detail how to choose, care for, and milk a cow. Containers for milk needed to be kept meticulously clean by scalding. Markham suggested making butter on Tuesday and Friday afternoons, since most towns held markets on Wednesdays and Saturdays, so any surplus could be sold. Touching on making cheese next, Markham reminded his readers that only sluttish, coarse women would hang their cheese to drain on the corner of the chimney.

Most cheese was made with milk fresh that morning and was called new cheese. Various other types could be made, including a cream cheese and a summery nettle cheese. Markham advised that whey, the leftover residue from cheese-making, should be offered to the poor as a nutritious drink or else mixed with oats and given to pigs and chickens. A posthumous publication attributed to Hannah Woolley (1622–1675), *The Complete Servant-Maid* (1677), was less benevolent, and directed that a dairy maid should, 'see that your hogs have the whey, and that it be not given away to gossiping and idle people, who live merely upon what they can get from servants.'

Another part of the housewife's role was making malt from barley. Malt is a fermented grain that was brewed into spirits, beer, and malt vinegar. Women were usually in charge of making malt and Markham was very keen that this should be recognised as women's work, done indoors by the housewife and her maids. The grain was laid out on the floor of a malt house or a special room in sheltered conditions and encouraged to germinate. Malt-making was an art as the grains had to go through several processes, including soaking and drying in a kiln, and took several weeks of careful management. Beers could be ready to drink after two weeks, but were best laid down for a year, and strong ales took a little longer to brew.

The housewife would be expected to choose and order in other supplies as needed. Wine was bought in and so Markham's book taught her how to recognise the markings on wine barrels, which indicate the quantity and strength of the contents. Making all of the basics of the early modern diet required having not only the skills but the equipment; for many people building their own brew house wasn't an option, so beer was bought from the local brewery. Equally, many houses only had the option of an open fire and grate which made spit roasting, frying and boiling possible but not bread baking, for example, and many people habitually bought a fresh penny loaf on a daily basis.

Spinning and Sewing: Clothing and Household Linens

After feeding her family, Markham explained that the housewife needed to be able to make clothes to keep her family either warm or cool as the seasons dictated, but also to keep them smartly turned out. Linen was thought essential for keeping your skin clean and healthy, as it was believed to draw dirt and sweat away from the body. An under-layer of linen, a smock or shift, was worn by both sexes all the time for this reason.

Linen was made from hemp or flax, which the housewife could grow herself. It was harvested at the end of summer, pulled out at the roots, not cut down like corn. Hemp had to go through a number of processes, including being boiled and heckled (combed and straightened), which Markham advised doing twice. It was then spun into balls before being sent to a professional weaver to be turned into cloth, then the fabric would be bleached in various compounds to turn it white and finally worked into garments.

Since nothing was wasted in this society, even the lower grade woollen fleeces unsuitable for clothing were sorted and retained for making bed covers. While housewives were expected to spin and work threads at home, from 1622, to protect the textile industry, women were restricted to making only sufficient cloth for their own households, and banned from selling it on for extra income.

Selected high quality wool would be sent out for dyeing, although Markham also offered recipes for home dyeing. He described the traditional colours, and explains how madder and bran could be used to make reds. He then revealed how to dye your wool 'puke' colour, a deep bluish black, made from copper and other metals. Wool then had to go through several stages such as greasing, carding (combing), spinning, and warping. Like hemp or flax, the balls of wool were then normally handed over to a weaver to turn into cloth. Other balls of thread could be kept back to knit into things like hose, or stockings, which both sexes wore.

As well as clothes, everything made from fabric in the average early modern household had to be home-made. Linen was cut to size and hemmed to make cloths, or clouts, for a multitude of household uses, such as towels, which were cut and reused for other purposes as they wore out. Beds generally had a linen sheet on top of a mattress, resting on a wooden frame strung with crossed ropes. The ropes needed to be tightened periodically as they became slack and this is where the saying 'sleep tight' comes from, since a firm base gave a better night's sleep.

Mattresses were often laid on a woven rush matt over the ropes, and were made from feathers stuffed in a canvas bag if you could afford it, straw if not. While the poor only ever had the option of a straw bed, Jacques Guillemeau's 1612 guide to childbirth sensibly advised wealthier women to use disposable straw beds for giving birth, rather than ruining their fine feather beds. Straw was not just made from dried grasses but almost any crop, such as by drying the stalks and the foliage left after a pea harvest to make 'pease-straw.'

Beds, known as 'tester-beds' had curtains around them, which were often embroidered. These curtains often represented the only privacy a married couple might have, since they routinely shared a bedroom with children and servants. Beds needed to be slept in to remain aired and in larger households it was usual for maids to be ordered to sleep in the main bed for a few nights, if the householder was away, to make sure it was freshly aired for their return.

A 'best' bed was kept in wealthier households for visitors to use which is why William Shakespeare bequeathed his second-best bed to Anne: this second-best bed was their marital bed. Women regularly shared beds with their maids if their husbands were away, which makes a lot of sense in draughty houses. As well as an under- and over-sheet, the bed would have had a woollen coverlet. In place of wallpaper, homes often had woollen tapestries covering the walls to keep heat in.

Sweeping, Washing and Rubbing: Cleaning the Early Modern House

Interestingly, the role we now most commonly associate with the term 'housework,' cleaning, does not feature in Markham's housewifery guide, other than in brief comments stressing the importance of keeping clean. Most domestic chores were the responsibility of the maid or the lowliest person in the household, sometimes a poor relation, although Royal Navy chaplain, Henry Teonge (1621–1690) stated in his diary in 1675 that, 'the chiefest care of the neat housewife was to keep their rooms free from all manner of dust by sweeping, washing and rubbing them.'

Cleaning was arguably more straightforward at that time, since for most people a house was relatively uncluttered and basic. Most floors were of compacted earth and, while this could be dusty, it just needed a regular sweep to keep clean. Larger houses covered their floors with rushes, either loose or woven into mats, and these could be changed regularly. The rushes might be sprinkled with dried herbs and flowers, so that as they were crushed underfoot they released a pleasant scent.

The piece of wood known as the threshold of a door first came into being to keep the rushes from drifting outside. Alice Thornton described how she tripped over the threshold of her house at Hipswell when she was around 30 weeks pregnant, on 1 September 1657. While rushes might not be used upstairs, there would be floorboards which needed a sweep and might be mopped too. Carpets were not used on the floor but on walls or tables as decoration.

Soap was bought in blocks, as making it at home was a messy and smelly process. Animal fat was rendered or purified and then boiled with wood ash (lye). It had to set for several weeks before being used. The same soap was used for cleaning, laundry and washing the body. A small amount was cut from the block and melted into warm water. Because it was a costly item, employers constantly exhorted laundry or scullery maids to be economical with it. Sand was used to scour pots and the kitchen table was also scrubbed with it too.

A particularly repetitive and unpleasant household job was the regular emptying of the chamber pots. Larger households would keep a 'necessary maid' just for this task, but normally a scullery maid would be responsible for washing the pots out, after she had scrubbed and scoured all the household pots and pans. More wealthy houses also had close–stools, a form of commode, which resembled a box with a padded seat and lid, containing a pot. The pots were usually emptied into the outdoor privy, although some houses had a soil heap piled up outside – a source of constant complaints in the neighbourhood courts of built–up areas, for obvious reasons.

Toilets or privies were also known as necessary houses, houses of office, houses of easement, or jakes. In the countryside they might be built over a stream to remove the waste, but in cities the waste dropped into cesspits. It was usual for several houses or a street to share a privy. Urine was collected in a bucket and used to bleach linen or sold to the local tannery, providing an extra source of income for poorer families.

Luckily for servants, the job of emptying privies was considered a specialist job, that of the night–soil men. They came at night and emptied the privy by lowering buckets into the pit and scooping out the waste, removing it in barrows which they often had to wheel back through houses, as there was no separate access to the rear of many homes. Hiring the night–soil men was expensive and even the middle classes put it off as long as possible. In October 1660 Samuel Pepys (1633–1703) described going down into his cellar and stepping into a pile of excrement, where his neighbour Mr Turner's toilet had overflowed and seeped through the wall to the Pepys' house.

Like urine, other left–over household commodities were recycled wherever possible. Food waste was fed to the pig, an animal most households would rear as a source of winter food; the remains of tallow candles would be added to the scraps fed to the dog, but other items of household waste were left outside the house for the 'scavengers' employed by the city authorities to take away at night. This included oyster shells, animal bones from cooking, turnip heads, dust, and even dead pets. Every householder was responsible for keeping the road outside their house swept and could be fined for not cooperating. In a letter to the Bailiff of Buckingham it was suggested that residents of Kensington should be required, 'twice every Week [to] sweep before their Houses and Buildings, and take up the Dirt ready for the Scavenger, or other Officer,' or face a fine of 3 shillings and 4 pence.

There was no universal standard or conventional approach that all household management books advocated, even though there were common themes, and there were also clear differences in regional practices and customs in early modern housewifery. Henry Teonge, who came from Warwickshire, noted his amazement when his ship stopped at Deal to see the locals bleaching and drying linen on the white beach, while shunning the green grass nearby. He also noted that housewives spread sand on the floorboards after they had swept them.

Obviously a woman's social and financial position would have affected how much she was involved with household activities on a daily basis and the level of supervision required of her. Yet, it is clear that even if she didn't do the work herself, she was expected to know how it was done in order to make sure her household was run in the best, most cost-effective way.

Chapter Two

Women in Business:
The Economic Lives of Early Modern Women

One aspect of the early modern era that often surprises people is the extent to which women participated in the household economy. One probable reason for this is that from the eighteenth century, with the rise of the new middle classes, there was a growing separation of work as a man's world and the home as a woman's realm, a division which simply didn't exist before this period.

In early modern times married couples functioned much more like a team in terms of income, albeit under the assumption that the wife's contribution was of a lower status, and invariably lower paid, than her husband's, and they very often worked together from the home. Unmarried women were obliged by law to work. The 1543 Statute of Artificers stated that women between the ages of 12-40 could be obliged to go into service in any manner the local authorities deemed fit, although it seems likely that only those women who would become a financial burden on the parish would see this enforced. This chapter examines some of the jobs and trades that occupied women in the early modern period.

For women, paid work was done in addition to household management duties. Washerwoman Mary Collier (1688–1762) made this point precisely in a poem of 1739, 'The Woman's Labour.' Her poem describes taking her children with her to work in the fields and how at the end of the day women, 'must make haste, for when we home are come, / We find again our Work has just begun.' Collier was in the bottom tier of society as a manual labourer in the fields and a washer woman. She described how she had to walk to work through all weathers, hours before dawn, to the house where she was employed:

But when from wind and weather we get in,
Briskly with courage we our work begin;
Heaps of fine linen we before us view,
Whereon to lay our strength and patience too;
Cambricks and muslins, which our ladies wear,
Laces and edgings, costly, fine, and rare,
Which must be washed with utmost skill and care;
With Holland shirts, ruffles and fringes too,
Fashions which our fore-fathers never knew.
For several hours here we work and slave,
Before we can one glimpse of day-light have;
We labour hard before the morning's past,
Because we fear the time runs on too fast.

Collier described vividly how her mistress would constantly demand she use less soap and hot water to lower the costs, while keeping the standards high. She described how her hands would become so raw that blood, as well as sweat ran down her fingers. Collier's verse aptly portrays the realities of working life for a woman of her social class. Of course, Collier was generalising to make her point, and there are accounts of men helping in the home and looking after the family and household during their wife's lying-in, following childbirth, for example.

Some of the occupations a woman might hold are now unfamiliar, such as the wig maker that scientist Robert Hooke (1635–1703) referred to in his diary. Hooke noted in February 1675 that he paid 'the periwig woman at Gresham College Gate 2s 6d.' Periwigs required a lot of maintenance and had to be cleaned, re-curled and deloused as the need arose. More common occupations for women are given in an account of a children's home, a 'general nursery, or college of infants' set up by magistrates in Middlesex in 1686.

The account describes a matron who was in charge of the domestic sphere; a cook; a school mistress employed to teach girls the catechism, to read and to say prayers; a seamstress who taught the girls to make all the clothes and linen for the household; a nurse to tend the sick and weak infants, who might have employed a number of assistants; a laundress; and several chamber women whose responsibilities were 'to Wash and keep Clean all the Lodgings, make the Beds, and to do other necessary Work there.'

Training and Apprenticeships

For girls in the social groups above Mary Collier, a period in domestic service was common. This period functioned as an apprenticeship to the role of housewife and supplied training for marriage. Girls in service would carry out the daily drudge needed to keep the house running: fetching water, beating rugs, scrubbing the table with sand on a daily basis to keep it sanitary, emptying the family's chamber pots and so forth.

Girls, like boys, could also take an apprenticeship into a trade. Many indenture forms for apprentice girls survive, despite the fact that they were often torn in two with each party keeping a half and the matching of the ragged seam proving each had half the original document. An apprenticeship was normally for a seven-year period, between the ages of 14 and 21, but could be longer. The apprentice's family would normally have to pay a fee for their child to be trained, and although the child would not be paid, their board and lodging would be provided and all their tools, along with the expectation of proper training in their chosen profession. Girls were apprenticed in a range of occupations, from seamstresses to midwives.

Apprenticeships, both in the shape of informal service and trades, were one of the reasons why the average age of marriage in the late seventeenth century was higher than among the aristocracy, at around 26, while teenage matches were more typical in the upper ranks. A young person would need to have completed their apprenticeship before setting up their own household, and a condition of apprenticeship was that marriage was forbidden. The former apprentices would then work to establish themselves within their trade before they were in a position to marry. Mary Woodforde's record in her diary of a household servant Ann leaving her service after 13 years to marry is, therefore, very typical if Ann had gone into service in her early teens.

Dame Schools and Horn Books: Teaching Children

Women who could read would teach their children, often with a hornbook, a sheet of paper covered with the alphabet or the Lord's Prayer pasted on to a paddle made of bone or horn. Many more people could read than write and the growth of reading was connected to the Protestant Reformation, which had encouraged people to read the Bible for themselves and to form a personal relationship with God. Even by the mid–eighteenth century, fewer than half of all women could sign their names, but many would have been able to read to a rudimentary level.

Some women taught groups of children who came to their homes, for a fee. These became known as dame schools, because 'dame' was the honorary title given to teachers. Both boys and girls might attend dame schools. In 1714 at the age of four, lexicographer Samuel Johnson (1709–1784), went to Anne Oliver's school, run from her cottage on Dam Street in Lichfield, Staffordshire. Hannah Woolley, the author of books of household management, ran a school in Hackney in Middlesex, where she also provided medical treatments.

Hannah Allen (b. 1638) a gentleman's daughter from Staffordshire was sent at the age of 12 to live with her aunt and uncle in the Parish of Aldermanbury in London, and attend a school there. This was common for girls of Allen's class, and the school she attended possibly also admitted boarders. A number of girls' boarding schools were established in Chelsea, then a large village which had already become a fashionable place to live.

Theodosia Alleine (1630–1669) ran a large boarding school for several years in her home near Taunton, to support her family after her preacher husband lost his living. By her teaching she noted, 'his income was for that time considerably enlarged,' showing how her remuneration was automatically considered her husband's money. In her biography of Joseph Alleine, Theodosia described how she was used to hard work, having 'been always bred to work,' and that she had 'seldom less than Twenty, and many times Thirty' in the household and 'usually Fifty or Sixty of the Town and other Places.'

'Goody Nurse, Doctress or Midwife': Medical Women

To train as a midwife involved serving an apprenticeship and experienced midwives were expected to train the next generation too. On the Continent midwives had to complete an oral examination before doctors, but in England the Church had the authority to licence midwives. Ecclesiastical licensing of midwives was more strictly enforced at some times more than others during the turbulence of the seventeenth century; the practice drifted to an end in the first decades of the eighteenth century, rather than being formally rescinded.

When a young woman had completed her midwifery apprenticeship and acquired proficiency, she needed a number of witnesses to attest to her good character and her skill in assisting at births. She then had to swear an oath before a bishop, promising to work for rich and poor alike, and not to give precedent to richer clients. She also had to take an oath that she would not use 'witchcraft, charms, sorcery, invocation or other prayers,' nor allow any child she delivered to be baptised in the Catholic faith. One of the reasons a midwife was a prestigious job in the eyes of the Church was that in extreme cases where the baby was unlikely to survive during the time it would take to send for a vicar, the midwife had to baptise the baby herself.

The job could be a lucrative one: whereas delivering a poor woman reliant on the parish might only incur a fee of a couple of shillings, other births could be charged at a guinea or more. The midwife would also be paid a small sum or a gift in kind from the baby's godparents. Samuel Pepys recorded giving the midwife 10 shillings on the birth of one of his godchildren.

Women were involved in all aspects of healthcare in the home, and for some this extended beyond their own household. Although women were not allowed to study medicine at university and so could not become qualified doctors, and indeed it was not until 1865 that Elizabeth Garrett Anderson famously became the first English woman to hold a medical degree, women often provided professional medical care. In Elizabethan London several women were even prosecuted by the College of Physicians for working as unlicensed practitioners.

Women might sell herbal cures and advice from home, work as a nurse or, as in a few instances, operate as a barber-surgeon. During the Civil War women, like Lady Anne Halkett (1622–1699), worked on the battlegrounds, bandaging and tending the wounded. An anonymously published pamphlet designed to sell the author's cures, described a number of diseases, and lamented that a woman with a lump in her breast would show it to every 'Goody Nurse, Doctress or Midwife' when she was seeking a diagnosis. The author naturally suggested that rather than consulting these women the sufferer should buy his cream: 'The Price of this Liniment is Five Shillings the Gallipot [*small jar*].'

Sometimes these women were itinerant workers, much like the travelling mountebanks who went from town to town. Lady Elizabeth Delaval noted in her memoir that when she was 16 she had had a troublesome tooth mended by an old lady who called at her home. Recalling the episode from the mid-1660s, Elizabeth described how she had been in unbearable pain 'which a poor unlearned woman (with God's blessing) promises me ease of.' The woman decided that the real problem was due to the presence of worms in Elizabeth's tooth (a commonly accepted cause of toothache, as the worm was thought to wriggle in a tooth cavity, irritating the nerve).

As the daughter of an earl, Elizabeth did have access to physicians but chose to let this woman help her, which she was aware would raise a wry smile in some quarters: 'I know, tell this now to any learned doctor of physic and he will rather smile at my simplicity, for expecting it to be eased by this woman's skill, than not believe her more likely than to cheat than cure me.' The cheat Elizabeth referred to was a well-known trick, whereby some tiny pieces of white lute sting were placed in the quill that was used to apparently tease out the worms. The 'worms' were then tipped out to show that the cure had worked. Elizabeth took pains to explain that she and her servants checked the quill before it was used, claiming it was impossible that she was gulled, and tooth-worms really were extracted this way, curing her pain.

Popular culture often showed the women who worked in the practical areas of health as unruly figures of fun, and even allowed for the charge of witchcraft to be levelled at them, particularly in the earlier part of the period. There was a class distinction too, as elite women were expected to act as doctors to their household and provide medicines and care as part of their duties. The difference perhaps, is that they did this as an act of benevolence and did not take payment for it.

However, given the limited access to doctors who, as well as being quite rare, were beyond the financial means of most people, these women 'doctoresses' were clearly providing a much needed service.

Printers, Publishers and Booksellers

A good many female printer/publishers are listed in seventeenth century books. They might have inherited their businesses upon the death of a husband, because if a tradesman died it was usual for his wife to be admitted into his trade guild in his place and carry on the business. It was forbidden for a wife to practise her husband's trade if he was present, however, so she could only legally take over if he was away on business, or at war, for example. Like other specialist trades, it seems to have been normal that the wife kept the books and ran the retail side of the printing business, while her husband did the manual work of running the presses. After she took over the ownership of the business this might have continued, with apprentices or journeymen still running the workshop.

In this period a printer was often also a publisher, and women published a wide range of books. Hannah Allen inherited her husband Benjamin's printing business on his death in 1646. The business seems to have thrived, as she published over 60 books and pamphlets, but when she remarried in 1651 to a former apprentice, Livewell Chapman, her name almost disappears from the records, as the business then became his. However, a Hannah Chapman is listed in the Stationers' Company poor book from 1678 to 1705, which suggests that she lived for many years on benefits from her trade guild.

Another printer/publisher was Sarah Griffin, who carried on the family printing business for over 20 years after the death of her husband Edward. Sarah published John Oliver's *Present for Teeming Women,* a book of prayers considered suitable for a pregnant woman to use, which was also commissioned by a woman, bookseller Mary Rothwell, in 1663. The range of books Sarah printed included a pamphlet about love-sickness, *Lunaticus Inamoratus or, The Mad Lover* (1667); religious books in Latin (1661) and some texts in Welsh, including one by Lewis Bayly (1656); George Castle's reworking of Galen's medical treatises (1667); political tracts about the Civil Wars and the Restoration of the King in 1660.

Like most printers, Sarah acted as a book seller too and one anonymous book called *A Letter from a Person of Quality in Edenburgh to an Officer of the Army* (1657), printed for Thomas Hewer, advertised that it was to be sold 'at her house in Eliot's Court in the little Old Baily.' She held the contract for printing George Rose's *Almanac* for a number of years in the late 1660s and early 1670s on behalf of the Company of Stationers, which suggests that her work was held in high regard.

Rag Women and Manufacturies: Textile Workers

The textile trade was the second largest industry contributing to the national economy after agriculture. Tens of thousands of men, women, and children were employed in trades and tasks allied to this industry. Wool and linen were the main cloths; some silk was imported but cotton was not yet used in any quantity. There were many skilled jobs concerned with producing the materials to make clothes and household linens. Like the majority of all the trades before the Industrial Revolution, most textile workers worked from home. These included specialist lace-makers, ribbon weavers, silk-weavers, spinners (spinsters in the original sense), weavers (from where the surname Webster derives), and dyers.

As linen became more popular during the period, some landowners experimented with 'manufacturies' or turning outbuildings into dedicated weaving areas in which people could work. The travel writings of Celia Fiennes (1662–1741) note this happening in Yorkshire in the later seventeenth century. The wool trade, in all its various aspects, was subject to high taxation from the crown and was notoriously badly paid. Most people out of necessity made their own clothes, but certain parts had to be bought in. Stays, or corsets, for example, needed to be fitted and tailored and so were bought from a specialist.

Home spinning or piecework, like carding (combing) of wool might be a supplementary trade that the wives and children of a husbandman (or small tenant farmer) did to bring in additional income during the leaner winter months, a time when fewer hands were needed on the land. Lace-making was another laborious and poorly rewarded task. Women often learned how to do it, but it was also a specialist occupation. Bobbin lace was made by a type of plaiting or weaving, in which thread was wound around bones and then pins were used to create the holes of the desired pattern, whereas needle lace was created by a needle and single thread. Women called 'rag-women' sold lace door-to-door.

Laundresses

As well as working, as Mary Collier did, in a large house where the laundry was done by household servants, some women took in washing at home.

This was not just the laundry of the wealthy but from ordinary people, who might not have the facilities to boil up a pile of washing at home, so took linen to a laundress on an occasional basis. For the merchant classes too, sending out clothes to be laundered and starched was essential.

After washing, laundry was spread on hedgerows to dry. This system was presumably used for practical reasons, but it has been shown that the effect of the sun and the chlorophyll in the foliage helps to bleach the cloth. Bristol midwife Sarah Stone referred to several of her clients working as laundresses in her midwifery book from 1737. She even described how, because of the need to get back to earning an income – since these women often didn't have the funds to support the 'woman's month,' or the whole month off work that women traditionally took to recover from giving birth – some of her women were back working in a couple of weeks.

In the Fields: Women and Agriculture

If a woman was married to a farmer with land of a sufficient size to support the household, then in addition to running the home and family, her role would often be to keep chickens for sale, along with their eggs and make the butter and cheese to sell at market. She would also keep a few pigs, and make meat products to sell. In summer, she might also have made cider from her orchards, both for sale and for the household. A farmer's wife usually had servants to help in her day-to-day tasks and ran her side of the farm like a small business.

In the days before the eighteenth century Enclosure Acts, people had the right to graze animals on common-land and so a tenant farmer – who had some land but still had to work for wages on other farms – might keep a cow or some sheep. His wife would tend these while he was out at work, in addition to her other jobs. She would also keep a kitchen garden to supply as much of their own needs as possible. At harvest time she and her children would work the land, as Mary Collier described.

Labourers were at the bottom of the agricultural chain and were employed on a very small daily rate, which could include some food (bread and beer). Their families worked on the same basis, and apart from at harvest time, when they and their children were in demand, they might get work on the land weeding the crops by hand. This was back-breaking work and very poorly paid.

At the end of the day in the fields, the labourer's wife would then have to start her second job: 'We must make haste, for when we home are come, / We find again our work has just begun.' Mary Collier explained that in the evening she had to make her:

> *... House in order set;*
> *Bacon and Dumpling in the Pot we boil,*
> *Our Beds we make, our Swine we feed the while;*
> *Then wait at Door to see you coming Home,*
> *And set the Table out against you come:*
> *Early next Morning we on you attend;*
> *Our Children dress and feed, their Clothes we mend;*
> *And in the Field our daily Task renew.*

Retailers and Shopkeepers

While a farmer's wife would sell her produce at market, women also ran a large variety of shops. Increasing numbers of women became shopkeepers as the seventeenth century progressed. An advert for his scurvy pills published by M. Bromfield in 1694 lists all the shops where his tablets, sealed in tin boxes of 40 for 3 shillings or 20 for 18 pence, could be bought. These included several shops all around London run by women:

> *Mrs. Stanley, seamstress at her shop without Moorgate; Mrs. Green, seamstress near Fauntain Stairs on Redrif Wall; Mrs. Mary Tonson, stationer at Gray's-Inngate next Gray's Inn Lane; Mrs. Harding, chandler over-against the Mount in White-Chapel; Mrs. Banbury, at her shop in Westminster Hall, near the Common-Pleas.*

In the same vein, Anthony Daffy's medicinal elixir was offered for sale in Mrs Low's strongwater-shop at the Corner of Green-street near Leicester Fields; from Mrs Johnson at Johnson's coffee-house, near St James's

Church; by Mrs Mary Powell, a seamstress, at Greys-Inn-gate in Holborn; and from Mrs Bently, a bookseller in Covent-Garden.

Other shops commonly run by women included bakeries selling breads and filled pies, cake shops, and meat and fish shops. Butchers' and bakers' wives would walk through the streets selling their produce from baskets. Women might also sell asses' milk in the street, straight from a donkey which she would milk on demand for her customers into their own containers. This milk seems to have been preferred in towns and cities to cow's milk, as it was considered better for you. Cow's milk cheeses and butter made in the country would be sold in markets. Towards the later seventeenth century, coffee shops grew up, often run by women but frequented exclusively by men.

Women also ran taverns and bars known as ordinaries. A pub in Surrey run by 'ale-wife' Eleanor Rumming famously became the subject of a bawdy poem by John Skelton. This disparaging poem claimed that after 40 years in the trade Eleanor's Lincoln green hood (or headdress, worn over the coif or linen cap) was threadbare. Eleanor brewed her own ale, as many taverns did, but it was mocked in the poem for being too frothy or 'nappy.' Towns and cities were often loud, vibrant places filled with chatter, as people met or bought and sold goods in the streets.

Shops were known by the painted symbols on the sign outside them. In an age with low literacy and no house numbers, pictorial signs were needed. A vintners or strong-water shop, like Mrs Low's, might have had a holly brush (resembling a witch's broom) on the sign outside. The best shops, of course, were advertised by word-of-mouth, hence the popular saying, 'good wine needs no bush.'

Some of these female shopkeepers were widows who had taken over the family business on the death of their husband. While all good housewives knew how to make most of their budget, if they were working at a spinning wheel all day then they might not have had time to cook and so might buy in more food than a housewife with more time. The variety of foodstuffs for sale shows that there was a market. A simple meal in an ordinary or tavern would only cost 1½ pence and so was within many people's means. In the country, apart from on market days, the range of goods for purchase was more limited and households were obliged to be more self-sufficient.

What is clear from this chapter, however, is that working for money was something all but the highest ranking women were 'bred to do,' as Theodosia Alleine put it. Women held a range of positions, and until the rise of the middling sort, the future middle-classes, during this period, the notion of a woman having no other occupation than that of housewife was not usual.

Chapter Three

Childcare:
Raising Children from Infancy to Adulthood

R aising children was a significant part of most women's lives in this period. Sadly almost a third of children died before reaching adulthood, with most deaths occurring before the age of five. It is perhaps unsurprising therefore that historians once argued that women couldn't afford to form an emotional bond with their children and so were emotionally distant from them. This interpretation, however, has been challenged by many recent commentators.

Ann Hulton's bitter cry after the death of a newborn child on 29 July 1689, after a labour which nearly cost her own life, shows the extent to which the love for a baby was seen as mitigation for the ordeal of labour: 'O Adam, Adam! What hast thou done! My comforts are taken away before I had well received them: was it all lost labour?' In the case of older children, the heartbreak of early modern parents reveals the grief the loss of a child caused.

In her memoir, Lady Ann Fanshawe (1625–1680) described the death of her nine-year-old daughter who died of smallpox:

upon the 22nd of July, 1654, at 3 o'clock in the afternoon, died our most dearly beloved daughter Ann Fanshawe, whose beauty and wit exceeded all that ever I saw of her age. She was between nine and ten years old, very tall, and the dear companion of our travels and sorrows. She lay sick but five days of the smallpox; in which time she expressed many wise and devout sayings, as is a miracle for her years. We both wished to have gone into the grave with her. She lies buried in Tankersley church; and her death made us both desirous to quit that fatal place to us.

As Lady Ann wrote, the grief she and her husband felt laid so heavily upon them that they wished they could jump into the grave with their daughter. The following year Ann gave birth to another daughter and named her Ann too, in her deceased daughter's memory.

The Fanshawes were a higher-ranking family and they might have sent some of their children to be brought up in other households, which was then customary. The most common practice was for boys to be sent to the households of higher-ranking nobles, to ensure they got a good education and also gained a patron in the future. Girls too could be fostered out in this way, and if they were considered suitable, from the age of 14 might be offered a place at Court. Lady Elizabeth Delaval's half-brother, who was a cousin of the King, arranged for her to be placed in the household of Henrietta Maria, wife to Charles II, when she was 14. In Elizabeth's case this proved disastrous, as the bright lights at court turned her head and she ran up a fortune in debt.

Women's letters to their mothers and husbands about their children give glimpses of family life at this time. For example, in the later seventeenth century, Lady Elizabeth Hervey conjured up a cosy scene when, in a letter to her husband, she mentioned that their daughters were tucked up in bed alongside her, drinking hot chocolate. Brilliana, Lady Harley wrote regularly to her husband while he was away in Parliament to keep him up to date with their young family. Brilliana's letters are full of domestic detail, in one from 1627 she wrote that she has sent her husband a partridge pie in the same post, and reported to him that, 'I thank God, Ned and Robin are well; and Ned asks every day where you are, and he says you will come tomorrow.'

In December 1629 another letter shows how the Harley family had grown, with the addition of two more children, including a daughter named after her, who were seemingly full of the traditional winter colds and runny noses. Brilliana wrote to her husband that:

Ned has been ever since Sunday troubled with the rheum in his face very much. The swelling of his face made him very dull; but now I thank God, he is better, and begins to be merry [...] I must desire you to send me down a little Bible for him. He would not let me be in peace, till I promise to send for one. He begins now to delight in reading: and that is the book I would

*have him place his delight in. Tom has still a great cold; but he is not, I
thank God, sick with it. Brill and Robin, I thank God, are well; and Brill
has two teeth. Ned presents his humble duty to you, and I beg your blessing
for them all.*

Most of the first-hand accounts of raising children which exist are from
higher-ranking families because they were the ones with the means to
write down their experiences. This means there necessarily is a bias in this
chapter towards the upper ranks. However, the diaries of middle-ranking
fathers such as minister Isaac Archer (1641–1700), gentleman John Evelyn
(1620–1706), minister Ralph Josselin, and even wood turner Nehemiah
Wallington (1598–1658) show parents who took a detailed interest in their
children's well-being and who are much more even-handed and gentle with
their children than might have been supposed for the period, and while life
must have been much harder materially for children lower down the social
scale there is no reason to suppose their parents did not feel just as kindly
towards them.

For lower-ranking mothers, the pressures of earning a living meant that
there was little time to play or entertain children. Children did have the
chance to play though such as when in August 1631 Wallington recorded
how his three-year-old daughter Sarah went out to play with other little
children. Lower down the social scale, young children would work with their
mothers, as Mary Collier detailed in her poem (discussed in the previous
chapter) her children worked in the fields with her. Children working
alongside their parents or earning money running errands and such tasks
was a common sight.

This chapter looks at some of the aspects of mothering children beyond
infancy, and in particular nursing them through episodes of illness, which
is a regular feature of contemporary accounts. As the doctor and author
John Pechey put it in his 1697 book on childhood illnesses, parents were
considered the most suitable people to care for their children: 'it is best
and safest for Parents to have their Children under their own Eye and
inspection.'

Coughs, Itches, and Worms: Childhood Illnesses

A range of diseases were prevalent in the seventeenth century which now, thankfully, have been virtually or completely eradicated, due to vaccination programmes. Diseases were not conditional upon rank although treatments varied hugely dependent upon parents' means. Contagious diseases such as smallpox, measles, and whooping cough were once widespread. These conditions were largely treated with medicines and cordials designed to cool the body, in order to reduce the fever that was associated with them.

There are also numerous mentions in diaries and medical books of children falling down stairs or off stools and of them being scalded. Houses full of children and open fires could be hazardous places. Ralph Josselin recorded many childhood accidents amongst his brood and in one diary entry from February 1647, he noted how his toddler daughter Jane fell into the fire, but was rescued unharmed, only for her to stab her three-year-old brother Thomas in the eye with some scissors. Luckily they were both unscathed, but given that their mother had just given birth to her fourth, very sickly child, only days before, perhaps some sibling rivalry was at play.

Children were considered particularly susceptible to head lice. John Pechey wrote that lice were a problem in dirty adults who wore 'foul clothes,' but it was a condition that children regardless of rank or cleanliness could suffer from: 'this nasty disease is most familiar to Children, nor can Gentlemen's Children be free from them, for they breed in their Heads.' Pechey believed in the spontaneous generation of lice in children's hair, and explained that it was a troublesome condition which caused itching and, if untreated, could be fatal.

For Pechey, prevention was better than cure. If children were given a good diet excluding figs, they would be unlikely to 'generate' lice, he wrote. For those who already had them, a topical lotion made from boiling different herbs such as 'roots of Elecampane two Ounces, of Briony half an Ounce, of Beets, Mercury and Soapwort, each one handful, of Lupins one Ounce, Nitre, half an Ounce' could be made. Similarly, children were thought to generate worms in their stomachs and bowels, especially after eating fruit.

As well as lice, children and adults both suffered from infectious skin diseases like scabies. A mainstay of apothecary John Westover's business was dispensing 'girdles for the itch.' Ralph Josselin mentions it several times in his diary. Thomas Spooner wrote a book about 'the itch' in 1724, explaining that it differed from general itching and was a highly contagious disease with both wet and dry forms. Belts infused with mercury were used along with various skin creams to treat it, but it was obviously bothersome, given that people shared beds and so would re-infect one another. Spooner noted that the itch was second only to the plague in its infectiousness.

People would return to Westover to have their girdles refreshed or re-medicated, rather than run to the expense of buying a new one. In June that year Widow Arnell paid 3 shillings for the two itch girdles she bought, but would have been charged just one shilling each to have them refreshed with more mercury. Women would often barter with apothecaries like Westover for medicines and, on 26 March 1688, he noted that, 'Joan Adams of Wedmore had 2 girdles for the itch. She told me she would work it out at haymaking,' so would pay her bill in labour.

Troublesome teething was another childhood 'disease' familiar to many. Although perfectly natural, Pechey wrote that teething was classified as a disease because of the numerous symptoms accompanying it. Indeed Pechey even went so far as to say that, 'breeding of Teeth is often very dangerous, and many Children die of the Diseases and Symptoms that are occasioned thereby.' It wasn't just doctors who thought that teething could be fatal, Mary Roberts wrote in her journal that her eldest son John had died on the 15 May 1661, due to convulsions caused by cutting his teeth. Pechey suggested some soothing ointments for the gums and giving the child a candle to chew on; Katherine Packer, in 1639, also suggested using a wolf's tooth on a cord for the teething child to gnaw on.

Rickets, a condition now known to be caused by a lack of vitamin D, was considered to be a new disease in the period. Ralph Josselin feared his toddler Jane was sickening for it shortly after she was weaned in 1647. Pechey described how it only started 'sixty years ago' in the West of England. The disease seems to have first appeared in print in a bill of mortality in 1634. A few years later, Katherine Packer noted a cure for it in her commonplace book, which included boiling some liverwort in white wine to make a medicine. The condition was in fact known about from classical times, but it wasn't until 1650 that Francis Glisson (d. 1677) wrote a book dedicated to it.

For Pechey, the cure was purging to remove the excess phlegmatic humours in the child's body.

Children were thought likely to suffer from a number of other conditions due to the way their bodies were balanced. Under the humoral system children were thought to have an abundance of moisture within them, since the process of ageing was seen as a gradual drying out of the body. This excessive moisture could affect their digestion, leaving them, medical writers claimed, prone to nightmares. One book, *Children's Diseases, Both Outward and Inward* (1664), claimed that a bad diet could cause nightmares, so the mother must ensure that her child did not consume 'corrupt' or bad meat or milk.

Similarly, greed was thought to be characteristic of children and this too could cause disturbed sleep by sending vapours to the brain. This was easily diagnosed, because the child suffering from this condition would have 'stinking breath.' The cure was for the mother or nurse to be more careful with her own diet if the child was still breastfed, or to give them some honey to sooth the stomach and so aid sleep.

Another childhood 'disease' of which much was written was 'pissing the bed.' Unlike today, the term 'piss' was the everyday word for urination and not yet earned the vulgar connotations it now carries. Again, the cause was thought to be too much moisture in children's small bodies, and some doctors, therefore, advised that until a child was four it was best to do nothing about it. In older children various treatments were recommended, including ointments made from dried boar's bladder or hare's testicles.

It was generally accepted that children should be brought up to be quiet and respectful towards their parents. Contemporary writers, such as John Locke (1632–1704) in his book, *Some Thoughts Concerning Education* (1693), wrote that parents should avoid 'humouring and cockering [*indulging*]' their children as infants because, while such behaviour might be harmless in a young child, 'when they are too big to be dandled, and their parents can no longer make use of them as playthings, then they complain that the brats are untoward and perverse.' The seeds for a good adolescence were thought to be sown in good infant care.

Growing children provided just as many worries for mothers as infants, though. For example, matriarch Mary Woodforde, who lived to be 92, fretted about her children's behaviour and health in her diary. Trying episodes included when her eldest son Sam cut his finger badly at school and she had to wait anxiously for letters to hear how it was healing and whether it would function or not. It took nearly two months before she heard from Sam himself that the finger did not need to be amputated but was now 'useless.'

Mary didn't distinguish between her six natural children and the two stepchildren from her husband's first marriage, and prayed that God would keep her [*step*-]daughter Alice safe and in His 'fear and favour' during a visit she made to relatives in London.

Mothering Teenage Girls

The memoir of Elizabeth Isham (1608–1654) of Lamport Hall, gives an account of her teenage years, but also reveals the concerns her mother had over her health and behaviour. The main source of worry for Elizabeth's mother was that she was a solitary, bookish young woman. At this time excessive reading was thought to be damaging to girls' physical and moral health, and so her mother gave her responsibility for looking after some hens, with the promise of a reward if she did it well. This didn't prove the distraction her mother had hoped, as Elizabeth used the money she raised by selling her eggs to buy more books.

Like Elizabeth Isham, Lady Elizabeth Delaval, mentioned earlier, inherited her love of reading from her grandmother. She also described her love of reading novels in her journal, but by the time she came to write her memoir, she blamed the hours she had spent reading romances as one of the reasons she had not been as pious an adolescent as she now claimed to consider proper.

While there were a number of schools to which young girls might be sent as day students, it was normal for girls to be home educated, just sufficiently to be able to read, and many who learnt to read did not go on to learn to write. In addition to reading, girls would be taught household skills, such as needlework and embroidery, essential in a society where everything from clothing to household linens were hand-stitched. In his testimonial of the exemplary life of his step-daughter, Sarah Featherstone, who had died suddenly at the age of 15, Thomas Brown described how she had become proficient in the skills his wife had felt it appropriate for her to learn, including knitting, sewing, reading and writing. Higher-ranking girls would also be taught foreign languages, such as French and Italian, and might have dance and music lessons too. Yorkshire gentlewoman Alice Thornton recorded in her memoir that she had instruction in 'French, dancing and lute.'

The onset of puberty in girls was expected anywhere between the ages of 12 to 14. For girls who started their periods much earlier there was concern that this might signal that they were more sexual and that they would live a shorter lifespan. The main concern for parents, though, was when menarche was delayed. A huge amount of medical print was spent on discussions of late menarche, which was thought to be the main symptom of a condition known as 'greensickness.' The other symptoms of greensickness were lethargy and loss of appetite and pale skin.

In some respects this condition has much in common with the modern disease of anorexia nervosa, although the two are not exactly the same. Greensickness was considered to be a problem because under the humoral system it was believed that by the age of 14 a girl's body had finished growing, and had used up all her spare blood in growth, so she now needed to evacuate the excess. If she wasn't having regular periods, then the blood might be corrupting within her veins and making her ill. Greensickness was something Elizabeth Isham noted she had suffered from as a teenager and that just as she was growing out of it at 16, her sister started displaying the same symptoms.

There were many cures suggested for greensickness, including 'steel-water' or iron supplements, purging medicines, and letting blood from the ankle. The main cure, however, was thought to be marriage, when the action of sexual intercourse would stimulate the veins of the womb to bring on the elusive first period. If possible, worried mothers might take their daughters to spa towns, such as Tunbridge Wells, to drink the iron-rich waters believed to cure the condition. John Wilmot, the Earl of Rochester, included just such a family in his poem, 'Tunbridge Wells,' in which a worried mother is depicted talking to another woman about her daughter's condition. The second woman advises the mother to forget the water cure and to marry off the daughter quickly instead:

Get her a husband, madam:
I married at that age, and ne'er had had 'em;
Was just like her. Steel waters let alone;
A back of steel will bring 'em better down.

Rochester's poem, while crude, does hit on the nub of the mass concern about greensickness, which was the fact that unless a girl was menstruating she could not conceive and so fulfil her role in society as a mother.

Boys' Education and Health

There were just two universities in early modern England, at Oxford and Cambridge, which admitted only boys, and normally only higher-ranking boys, although there were some scholarship places. Diarist Samuel Pepys, the son of a tailor, did well at grammar school and was granted a scholarship at Magdalene College, Cambridge, graduating in 1654.

For Hannah Woolley, author of *The Gentlewoman's Companion* (1673), the gender inequality in children's education was a scandal:

I cannot but complain of, and must condemn the great negligence of Parents, in letting the fertile ground of their Daughters lie fallow, yet send the barren Noddles of their Sons to the University, where they stay for no other purpose than to fill their empty Sconces with idle notions to make a noise in the Country.

The sons of gentlemen and aristocracy were generally sent to university around the age of 14. There they would be taught by a personal tutor, employed by the family, under the auspices of the university. The aim was to complete their education but quite often they left without obtaining a degree, as that was not the prime purpose of a university education for a gentleman: networking and befriending those who would later be powerful within the upper echelons of society was the priority.

Many surviving letters sent from mothers to sons on their going away to university not only that show the strength of the parental bond but also how much mothers worried about their sons' behaviour when they were beyond their control. Mary Woodforde described in her diary how worried she was about rumours that her son had been caught up in some bad behaviour at boarding school in Winchester. In March 1687, she noted that her second son Jack and his friends were refusing to do their work, or to be whipped in punishment for their wrongdoing. Her husband immediately went to see his son at school and Mary received a letter which, 'gives me hope he has now humbled himself.'

This wasn't the end of the trouble for Mary, as the following week her older son, Sam, was claiming of 'dullness and indisposition to his studies,' and asked his mother to persuade his father to let him move schools. After much praying on the topic, the Woodfordes decided to send Sam to St John's College, Cambridge, although he was then 19, several years older than the normal starting age.

Other mothers worried about their sons' physical and moral health while they were at university. In around 1620 Alice, Lady Hatton (c1570–1630) wrote to her son Christopher (b. c1605), who was studying at Jesus College, Cambridge, saying that she missed him so much that she had to 'strive sometimes against the fond affections of a mother,' or she would be sending for him to come home all the time. The main theme of the letter is that Christopher should not get so caught up in college life that he might forget to pray regularly:

> *I must put you in mind of your chief duty, which is to God, which I charge you not to neglect, but to dedicate your first thoughts to Him constantly; read His word reverently; hear sermons; strive to take notes that you can meditate on them, without which you can never practise, which is the only end for which you were created, to know God's will and to endeavour to do it.*

Alice went on to advise Christopher not to be lazy, both for the sake of his health and because it was a sin. Mary Woodforde experienced the same anxiety about Sam, and wrote in her diary in August 1688 that he had come home from Cambridge, 'I hope bettered in his learning, and not drawn away from sobriety and honesty.'

Elizabeth, Viscountess Mordaunt (1633–1679) had similar concerns, as she recorded in her diary. Her eldest son Charles went off to Oxford when he was 16, on 23 March 1674. Lady Elizabeth wrote a prayer in her diary for his safekeeping, asking that the Lord send holy angels to watch over him to protect him from evil, but also to keep his mind on his studies 'enlighten his understanding,' and to keep him honourable, and also for him to gain 'favour in the sight of all.' As his mother, Elizabeth was concerned for Charles' soul and behaviour but also, touchingly, that people would like him and that he would be esteemed.

Another mother concerned about the spiritual and bodily health of a son at university is demonstrated in a letter by Brilliana, Lady Harley to her eldest son Edward (1624–1700), who she referred to affectionately as 'Ned.' In December 1638, while he was studying at Magdalen Hall, Oxford, Brilliana worried over a kidney problem she was concerned he might be suffering from. She wrote, 'Dear Ned, be careful to use exercise; and for that pain in your back, it may be caused by some indisposition of the kidneys. I would have you drink in the morning beer boiled with liquorice; it is a most excellent thing for kidneys.'

While her advice here is purely practical, earlier in the letter Brilliana had warned Ned to be 'still [always] watchful over yourself, that custom in seeing and hearing of vice do not abate your distaste of it. I bless my God, for those good desires you have, and the comfort you find in the serving of God.' Because she was concerned that he wasn't eating properly, Brilliana regularly sent down baskets of food for Ned. On one occasion she sent him a goat pie, 'because you have not that meat ordinarily in Oxford.'

While many of Brilliana's letters to Ned did remind him of his duty to keep his head down and study hard, their letters also show how close the mother and son were and often she sent him errands to run. Living in rural Shropshire, Brilliana didn't have the same access to shops as Ned did in Oxford, so she would send him notes to buy her the latest romantic novels; being fluent in French, she would ask him to find it in the original, if possible, rather than in English translation.

She also charged her young son with finding her a new mirror, telling him that 'if there are any good looking glasses in Oxford choose me one about the bigness of that which I use to dress myself in, if you remember it.' She reminded him to take care to choose one which gave a good clear reflection, 'a true answer to one's face,' because the quality of mirrors was then extremely variable. In the same letter Ned was charged with sourcing some blue and white fruit dishes to replace broken ones at home.

Lady Elizabeth Petty (*c*.1636–1708/10) wrote weekly letters from Ireland, where her husband Sir William was appointed the Surveyor, to her children in London, in which she was desperate to hear all about their lives, 'I would have you tell me everything you hear, and where you go, and who comes to see you, and what clothes you have.' Lady Hatton always signed her letters, 'Your very loving mother, Ales Hatton,' and Brilliana too always signed off affectionately and then gave her full name, which might seem overly formal but was the convention then.

In the vast majority of households where university was not an option, young men and some young women would undertake an apprenticeship to learn a trade, or go into the service of a wealthier family. It was normal for children of all social levels to move out of the parental home by their early teenage years, but this, of course, did not end their mother's concern for them. The tradition of Mothering Sunday was mentioned by soldier Richard Symonds (1617–1692) in his diarised account of the marches of the Royalist Army. The practice of returning to your 'mother church' or home church on middle Sunday in Lent was centuries old, and involved a reunion of extended family.

However Symonds wrote that in Worcester at least, this had begun to evolve into a celebration more familiar to us today. In spring 1644, Symonds noted how 'every midlent Sunday is a great day at Worcester, when all the children and godchildren meet at the head and chief of the family and have a feast.' By the late eighteenth century, this date was known as mothering Sunday and would become the one day in the year when older children in service were guaranteed time off to visit their parents and often take the simnel Easter cake associated with this celebration.

The experience of childhood and therefore mothering varied enormously based on the social rank of the individual family. The surviving accounts, however, show that parents worried over their children's health and sought to educate them to be well-mannered, religious adults. Even amongst the strictest Puritan households there is not a sense that children should be seen and not heard. Upper-ranking children were included in parents' lives, even when raised and educated away from home. And while the children of the lower ranks had to work from a young age, this was often alongside their parents.

Part II

Personal Care

Chapter Four

Food and Drink

F ood is always an important factor in gaining an understanding of people's lives during any historical period. Discovering how and what people liked to eat can allow us to see into aspects of their lives which other topics cannot illuminate. Food is necessary for life but it takes on much greater significance, becomes imbued with rituals and takes up a large part of our day in the planning and preparation.

Staple foodstuffs changed considerably during this era. At the beginning of the period, women had not yet heard of the potato, which was introduced to England in the 1590s, and used carrots and turnips instead, yet by the end of the century potatoes had become an everyday foodstuff. This century saw the introduction of tea, coffee, and tobacco. Sugar became increasingly available and affordable as the century went on, and it was perhaps not a coincidence that the term 'obesity' became naturalised into English from Latin during the seventeenth century.

The manner in which people ate changed too, as forks for dining came into use in this period. It was customary to use your own cutlery, normally just a spoon and a knife, and so people who travelled would take a set of cutlery with them for use when they stopped in taverns or at other people's homes.

A correct diet was also thought to be crucial to keep your humours in balance. In William Shakespeare's *Twelfth Night* Sir Toby Belch asks his friend Sir Andrew Aguecheek, 'Does not our lives consist of the four elements?' He replies, 'Faith, so they say, but I think it rather consists of eating and drinking,' an answer which pleases Sir Toby, who says, 'Thou art a scholar; let us therefore eat and drink' (II.iii). Food and drink were envisaged as one element within the six non-natural factors identified by Galen in the first century as affecting one's health and humoral balance. The remaining five consisted of: air that one breathes; sleeping and waking; emotions and the mind; evacuations, including sexual emissions; and movement.

The link between diet and exercise was perceived as the key to wellness during the period. In describing the English diet, sixteenth century historian Raphael Holinshed's *History of England* (1587) noted that because England was such a northerly region, the heat in the stomachs of its inhabitants was greater than for people who lived in hotter climes, due to English people breathing in cold air which the body had to work harder to warm up. He commented that, 'it is no marvel therefore that our tables are oftentimes more plentifully garnished than those of other nations, and this trade hath continued with us even since the very beginning.' The English love of food was world-renowned though, and a well-used French proverb stated that, 'the English dig their graves with their teeth.'

Holinshed wrote that the nobility, gentry and students at Oxford and Cambridge normally ate their first meal at 11 am, followed by supper at 5 pm. The merchant classes seldom ate much before midday and supped at 6 pm. Husbandmen usually ate at high noon, but had a long wait for their supper at 7-8 pm. Tellingly, Holinshed noted that the luxury of having set meal times did not apply to the poorest ranks, who lived hand to mouth, and who ate only sporadically, where and when they could afford to. The practice of eating two meals a day was advised by doctors following the teachings of Galen, because digestion was thought to be a long process and so it was considered unwise to eat again until all the medical stages of digestion had been completed.

Holinshed suggested that in the past people had eaten more often, with an additional breakfast in the forenoon and beverages in the evening after supper, but in the Elizabethan era, apart from some hungry young men who couldn't wait until dinnertime, most people just made do with two meals a day. Breakfast is mentioned in many contemporary books, however, which suggests that it was increasingly taken in some parts of the country, at least. Meals were to be consumed in silence within the homes of nobility and gentry, and diners were supposed to pay close attention to their plates to make sure they only ate a moderate amount and didn't overeat.

Holinshed also described how gentlemen and merchants' families had up to six dishes served in a meal when they had company but, if the family were dining alone then one, two or three dishes would suffice. Meals were not divided into starter, main and desert courses but sweet and savoury dishes were served together, as all the dishes were laid out at once, rather than eaten consecutively. Meals were served in courses especially on special occasions, but all courses had a mix of sweet and savoury dishes for diners to choose from.

Staples of the Early Modern Diet

While meat was an important part of the diet for those who could afford it, vegetables, grains, and pulses made up the majority of the meals ordinary people ate. Bread was not just served on its own, but could act as a plate, known as a trencher, to serve other foods upon, as an ingredient to thicken stews and pottages, a thrifty use for stale bread, or toasted on an open fire and eaten warm. The most common loaf baked at this time was a small, round, flat manchet loaf (a roll made with wheat flour). Bread was then made from rye and wheat flours, which were ground and sieved. The dough was kneaded by hand and then Gervase Markham advised putting it in a clean linen cloth and stamping on it. After an hour to prove it was cut into small loaves, then scored around the circumference to help it rise and pricked on the top.

Loaves made with barley, buckwheat, rye and other grains made a coarse, blackish-brown bread that would be given to anyone who worked in the household, with pure white breads reserved for the higher ranks. The hierarchy of breads even carried over into the city guilds and it was not until 1645 that the brown-bread guild agreed to unite with the white-bread guild. Most people bought in bread and a one pound loaf generally cost around a penny.

While salad vegetables and herbs were widely used in early modern cooking, fruit was treated with caution because of its cold, wet properties which were thought to unbalance your humours by making you too cold and wet, or phlegmatic. Uncooked fruit was generally thought to be bad for you. Both Yorkshire gentlewoman Alice Thornton and Sussex minister Isaac Archer noted in their memoirs that family members had died from eating melons. Similarly, in adolescence both Lady Dionys Fitzherbert and Lady Elizabeth Delaval blamed eating raw fruit for making them ill.

However, cooked fruits, like apples, were thought to be beneficial and fruit tarts were a popular choice. Apple pies were made in tall pastry cases, like a modern pork pie, and were not cut into slices for serving, rather the lid was removed, with custard poured inside and then everyone could dig in. Thomas Tryon's recipe for apple or pear tart begins by instructing the cook to line the tart-pan with a coffin of paste (pastry), dusted with a bed of sugar, then sliced pears or apple, followed by currants and lemon and topped with some cinnamon, more sugar, and with a walnut sized dab of butter, before being covered in another layer of pastry, varnished with egg wash and baked. After baking, the pie would be sprinkled with more sugar and some rose water, then it could be stored until needed.

Pottages were another classic staple food, and a pan of pottage could be kept on the go and refilled for days at a time as it was eaten. It was made by steeping oatmeal in water and then bringing it to the boil, and adding chopped herbs when it began bubbling. Tryon recommended smallage (wild celery), clivers (a sticky plant which grows in the wild), water-cresses, elder-buds and nettle-tops. After it was cooked through, the pottage was consumed at blood temperature as it was or strained and added to butter and bread.

Food was expensive to buy and could be used as a means of payment. Famines, such as those of the 1590s, caused by failed harvests would push up costs but at times of plenty food might be more affordable. Cost was the reason Samuel Pepys famously buried his wine stores and a parmesan cheese in his garden on 4 September 1666, as the Great Fire of London raged. The apothecary John Westover recorded several instances when he accepted food stuffs as part-payment of debts. In January 1688 Westover took half an acre of wheat from William Voules for treating his wife.

Westover ran a hospital alongside his shop and it is notable that the brother of one of his residents, Elizabeth Jeanes, paid less than a pound for all her clothing and linen for the year, but that her bill for 'tabling' or meal bill came to 9 pounds, 4 shillings, 7 pence and a farthing – Westover was meticulous in his record keeping. In this case Westover was probably referring to Elizabeth's bed and board as a single item, as this would be too much for her food alone, although tabling, strictly speaking, meant meals alone.

Meat was the most expensive element of any meal and so needed handling with care. It was normally boiled in a smaller pot within a big cauldron-like pot, rather than directly on the heat. If it was roasted, in larger households, this was normally done on a spit often turned by a small dog, whose job it was to run in a wheel hoisted above the mantelpiece as the meat cooked, to keep the spit turning. The dogs were known as 'turnspits.'

According to Holinshed, in Roman times it was considered bad luck to eat some animals, but now there were no restraints against any meat, either for religious or public order reasons. The exceptions were periods when eating meat was forbidden by the Church, such as on public fast days like Fridays or during Lent.

An early advocate of vegetarianism, Thomas Tryon, described in *The Way to Save Wealth* (1695) how people could live comfortably on 2 pence a day, if they followed his tips. He recommended 'flummery' for breakfast which consisted of steeped and boiled oatmeal. He suggested that some liked to take it with ale mixed in and others with cream, but he recommended having it with bread mixed in as a strengthening meal, especially in hot weather. Tryon also swore by 'hasty-pudding,' essentially a white sauce, made from wheat flour, milk, and butter. He added that putting in a touch of ginger made this dish particularly hearty.

Floured milk (2 quarts of milk mixed with a pint of water and some flour) was another staple for poorer people, perhaps with an egg mixed in if one was available. Most people kept hens and so Tryon suggested that floured milk with a hunk of bread and butter and some cheese would be sufficient to feed even a labourer for the day. Tryon offered several egg-based meals: boiled, scrambled, fried, omelette-style, and even egg pies, in which eggs are mixed with fruit and bread and butter and made into little pies.

Balancing the need to feed a family with the costs of purchasing food was a daily headache for many women and no doubt tips like those offered by Tryon were familiar to many housewives.

Special Occasions and Religious Feasts

Many religious holidays were celebrated with special dishes or an abundance of food for those who could afford it. Feasts or banquets associated with Church festivals punctuated the year. For example, Candlemas (2 February), Lammas (1 August, Harvest Festival), and Michaelmas (29 September), Christmas (25 December). These festivals were famously frowned on during the Interregnum under Oliver Cromwell, because of their links with Catholicism, from associations with 'mass' and from the rowdy feasting they usually brought about.

To disassociate the holy days from Catholicism, the term 'tide' was substituted for 'mass.' Robert Braithwaite was alert to the cynicism behind this, commenting in his *Whimzies* (1631) that, 'by changing masse into tide, they [*these holidays*] become of full force and vertue.' For Puritans such as Oliver Cromwell, Christmas should have been a time of quiet reflection, fasting, and prayer, not a party. In 1647 an ordinance was passed abolishing feasts, including Christmas, Easter, and Whitsun, as it declared that these celebrations had no Biblical authority.

The Long Parliament even sat on Christmas Day to prove its point, and tried to make shopkeepers and other tradespeople open on that day too. In compensation for the lost holy days, parliament declared that the second Tuesday of each month should be a public holiday, allowing servants a day off. Despite the laws, people appear to have continued marking Christmas much as they always did, and with the Restoration in 1660 all the laws of the Commonwealth were voided and the legislative clock was reset to pre-war times – and so Christmas was lawful once again.

Preparations for Christmas in the seventeenth century might resonate for women today. Diarist Samuel Pepys recorded how his wife stayed up half the night on Christmas Eve 1666, supervising preparations; he wrote in his diary on Christmas Day: 'Lay pretty long in bed, and then rose, leaving my wife desirous of sleep, having sat up till four this morning seeing her maids make mince pies.' Plum pottage and mince pies were a staple Christmas food and are usually mentioned together.

Randle Holmes' compendium for gentlemen, *The Academy of Armoury* (1688), lists the dishes that he would have expected in a Christmas banquet, served over two courses. The first course included:

Oysters, brawn, mutton stew with marrow bone, a grand salad, capon pottage, breast of veal, boiled partridges, roast beef, mince pies, mutton in anchovy sauce, sweetbreads, roasted swan, venison pasties, a kid with a pudding in his belly, a steak pie, chickens in puff pastry, two geese (one roast, one larded) [covered with bacon or fat while cooking], *roast venison, roast turkey stuck with cloves, two capons, and a custard.*

If guests had any room left after all that, the second course comprised:

Oranges and lemons, a young Lamb or Kid, Rabbits, two larded, a pig sauced with tongues, ducks, some larded, two pheasants, one larded, a Swan or goose pie cold, partridges, some larded, Bologna sausages, anchovies, mushrooms, caviar, pickled oysters, teales, some larded, a gammon of Westphalia [smoked] *bacon, plovers, some larded, a quince or warden pie, woodcocks, some larded, a tart in puff pastry, preserved fruit and pippins, a dish of larks, neats'* [ox] *tongues, sturgeon and anchovies, and jellies.*

Mince pies were made with meat, often ox-tongue, suet, and currants and other fruits, and served hot or cold. One satirical poem 'The Poet's Complaint' (1682) even uses them as a metaphor to complain that people no longer appreciate plays, 'I' th' City-shops they're thought profane, / As were Mince-pies in Cromwell's Reign.'

Christmas was a much longer celebration than nowadays, with celebrations lasting until Twelfth Night. Twelfth Night marked the beginning of Epiphany, when the three Wise Men arrived before Christ, which marked the end of the festivities. On this night people would go out wassailing, which had changed from the medieval custom and now took the form of drinking to everyone's health with spiced ale from a shared bowl. People might go out on the streets to drink one another's health in this way. A special fruit cake was also baked for Twelfth Night with a dried bean concealed in it, and the person who got the bean in their slice became the king or queen of the celebration for the night.

Hannah Woolley's 1686 *Accomplished Ladies Delight* offered a menu for a suitable Candlemas banquet, which was almost as elaborate as those served at Christmas, comprising four courses:

1. *A pottage with a hen, a Catham Pudding* [a suet pudding with bacon and onions], *chicken fricassee, a leg of mutton with a salad.*
2. *Shin of mutton, a shin of veal, a lark pie, a couple of pullets, one larded.*
3. *A dish of woodcocks, a couple of rabbits, a dish of asparagus, a Westphalia gammon.*
4. *Two orange-tarts, one with herbs, a bacon-tart, an apple-tart, a dish of bon-chriten* [Williams] *pears, a dish of pippins, a dish of pearmains* [pear-shaped apples].

A banquet often formed part of a wedding celebration. The wedding cake, known as the 'bride-cake,' was more like a bread cake made of wheat and barley. It had an important role in the ceremony, as the bride and groom each ate a piece of it to solemnise their vows. The party afterwards might include a mary-bone pie, which was filled with marrowbone and oysters, ingredients thought to be aphrodisiacs.

While the practice of 'bedding' a young married couple had almost ended by the end of the seventeenth century, some did still adhere to it and Samuel Pepys referred to it a few times in his diaries. On the 10 July 1660 he and his wife attended the wedding of Anne Hartlib, and stayed for the meal. Pepys had to return to some business but promised to return to see the bride bedded. Bedding was a rowdy custom carried out when the couple retired to spend their first night together and were escorted to their chamber by the wedding party, with much innuendo and ribald songs. The couple might be given some posset (milk curdled with alcohol such as ale or sweet wine) and sometimes gifts of money, before they were left alone and everyone else continued feasting.

The main celebration after a birth was at the end of the woman's month of recovery. Women normally did not attend their children's baptisms, as they happened within days of the birth, when the woman was still meant to be in bed. A woman went to be 'churched' with her midwife and gossips, friends and neighbours and then came home to a party.

Churchings had a reputation of being rowdy affairs, but this was true too of funerals. The wake was then the period between the death and the burial, when family and friends would sit with the body, often feasting and drinking and reminiscing. While the funeral itself was normally a sombre affair, with special black mourning clothing being worn from the seventeenth century, there might be a party afterwards too.

Over- or Under-Eating: Feasting and Weightloss

Even in the early modern period, medical texts offered advice for those who wanted to lose weight. Diets generally involved purging the system of excess and taking more exercise. Thomas Lupton's book *A Thousand Notable Things* (1579), included a diet he claimed to have devised himself, which he said was proven to work and, 'an excellent & approved thing to make them slender that are gross.'

He recommended that dieters consume three or four cloves of garlic with as much bread and butter as they liked, morning and evening. They should drink three 'good drafts' of water in which fennel had been steeped and strained. Lupton gave an example of a man who had successfully used the diet: 'I knew a man that was marvellous gross, and could not go a quarter of a mile, but was enforced to rest him a dozen times at the least: that with this medicine took away his grossness, and after could journey very well on foot.' A century later, the anonymous author of *The Ladies Dictionary*, published in 1694, gave weight-loss tips such as rubbing one's skin vigorously and bathing in claret.

A poem by Thomas Lodge (1558–1625) 'To his Mistress A. L.,' which appeared in his collection *A Fig for Momus* (1595), has weight-loss as its theme. In the poem Mistress A. L., who was probably based on Lodge's teenaged niece Anne, asks for advice about how to take away the 'pursiness [breathlessness] and fat' that she has been suffering from. Lodge's answer begins by explaining that there are two types of fat: natural and unnatural. The former is that which your body needs and naturally stores. In 1615, medical writer Helkiah Crooke had explained in his book of the body, that natural fat existed to defend the body, such as by acting in place of a cushion on your bottom, protecting the veins from drying out, and as a food source in times of famine. Significantly though, Crooke explained that it also serves to fill the gaps between the 'muscles, vessels, and the skin, that so the body might be plump, equal, soft, white and beautiful.'

As Crooke's comments suggest, a more likely danger was the threat of famine – there were at least three in the 1590s alone caused by bad weather and failed harvests – and then people could be less choosy than ordinarily about what they would like to eat. Thomas Tryon's book gave advice on how to take away the 'unsavoury Rank Taste of Pease, Beans, Beech-mast, Acorns, Chestnuts, Vetches [*a type of pea*], and such like.' This involved repeatedly boiling them, changing the water each time. Dried afterwards, they could be ground and made into breads or pastries.

The heart of all early modern health was seen as balance and moderation. *The Ladies Dictionary* explained that extreme thinness and extreme fatness were equal problems: 'bodies that are very lean and scragged, we must own, cannot be very comely: it is a contrary extreme to corpulency and the parties face always seems to carry Lent in it.' However, as Lodge's poem says, a healthy body which carried a covering of fat was preferable to being too thin: 'fat, sleek, faire, and full, / Is better liked, then lean, lank, spare, and dull.'

Staple Drinks

Beer was the standard drink throughout the period, drunk by everyone from small children upwards. It was low in alcohol and so called 'small beer,' normally brewed in March (Marchbeer) and generally considered in best condition if it had rested for a year. People did also drink water, and water was regularly added to wine, but small beer was the normal drink of choice. If bought, beer cost around a penny a quart (a quarter gallon, or two pints).

It is often said that people drank beer because the water wasn't safe but this is not always the case, although doctors did offer advice about which type of water to drink. John Archer, in *Every Man his own Doctor* (1671), wrote that, 'There is a great variety of Waters, all which are cold and moist, but the best is that which is pure and clear, by the sight, taste, smell.' Archer cautioned that the worst water was from still water, such as lakes and marshes which was thick and crude. This water upset the stomach, obstructed the bowels, and caused fevers, but if it was boiled, cooled and the sediment discarded, it would be safe to drink.

People were clearly alert to the types of water that were fit to drink and those that were not. In cities, of course, where water might be piped in lead pipes to a centralised pump, then the water might well have been distasteful and best avoided without boiling. People also drank asses' milk sold in towns by a dairymaid going door to door and milking the animal on demand. Possets, mentioned above, were popular drinks, and often taken medicinally as a fortifying drink. Caudle, a warm beverage made from thin gruel, mixed with wine or ale, sweetened and spiced, was drunk by the sick and women in labour, as a way of receiving some nourishment while they were weak.

In some southern parts of the country cider made from pressed apples and perry from pears was common, while elsewhere mead, made from honey, was produced. Brilliana, Lady Harley sent mead to her husband in

Parliament from their Herefordshire home, but Raphael Holinshed, for one, wasn't keen on it, calling mead a swish swash (wishy-washy) drink. Ale was strong beer, made without hops unlike standard beers, from which it was comparatively easy to get drunk. Wine was widely available, but significantly more expensive than other drinks and so was only drunk by the gentry.

Many different types of wines were available and the aristocracy had started using Venetian glass to drink out of, and even those lower down the scale would use inferior, but less expensive English glassware. Pewter tableware included goblets and, for the wealthy, silver tankards. Medics suggested that drinking from silver cups was the healthiest choice, although everyone else drank from horn or leather beakers, or earthenware pots. Posset was drunk from a porringer, a shallow, straight-sided cup with two handles. The two-handled cup became the fashion in the late seventeenth century.

Coffee, Tea, and Hot Chocolate

The first coffee-house opened in England in 1650. Men would meet there to drink, gossip, conduct business and read the newspaper. Women often ran and served in coffee houses but didn't frequent them. The fact that they were male domains probably led to a pamphlet decrying coffee being printed. *The City-wives' Petition Against Coffee* (1674) argued that, while England was formerly known as 'a paradise for women,' since the craze for coffee-drinking, England was in danger of being a paradise no more. Coffee, they claimed, was responsible for making men impotent and infertile, and incapable of performing their marital duties.

In the same year a response appeared, entitled *The Men's Answer to the Women's Petition Against Coffee, Vindicating their own Performances*, arguing that women made unreasonable demands on men and were altogether too lascivious. It is possible that both pamphlets were produced by the same person, perhaps a coffee house owner, and designed to drum up coffee sales.

Coffee was made with a third of a spoon of roasted and ground coffee powder per person, mixed in a glass of boiling water with sugar, then re-boiled and poured into individual porcelain dishes. The recipe described in *The Manner of Making of Coffee, Tea, and Chocolate* (1685) then advised, 'so let it be drunk by little and little, as hot as it can possibly be endured, but especially fasting.' This book made some extraordinary claims for coffee and strongly hinted that it could work as an abortifacient, as it suggested more than once that it was excellent for women who had stomach-ache because she hadn't had her period recently, especially if she was to drink a lot of it, as hot as she could bear.

Tea was sold in coffee shops too. Samuel Pepys recorded trying tea for the first time on 25 September 1660, after a meeting, when he 'did send for a cup of tea (a China drink) of which I never drank before.' The drink came into its own because it was the favourite drink of Queen Catherine of Braganza (1638–1705), who was used to drinking it in her native country of Portugal. Catherine came to England upon her marriage in 1662, bringing tea as part of her vast dowry. In 1687 a poem to Catherine by Edmund Waller was published, 'Of Tea, Commended by her Majesty.' The poem acknowledged Catherine's role in popularising the drink: 'The best of Queens, and best of herbs, we owe / To that bold nation which the way did show.'

Tea was made by pouring boiling water on dried leaves and waiting until the tea leaves sank to the bottom of the glass jug, before serving it. Tea was thought to have many medicinal properties, such as being good for the digestion and curing migraines. Both tea and coffee were sweetened with sugar, but neither had milk added to them at this time.

Hot chocolate was made with milk and eggs. Chocolate powder, which was sold in cakes, was melted into sweetened hot water and then milk and eggs were whisked in. The author of the tea and coffee guide also suggested a quicker chocolate recipe more suitable to businessmen with little time to spare, like himself, and more wholesome: 'whilst you set on the water to boil you must take a cake of *chocolate*, which you may either pound in the mortar, or rather grate it to a fine powder, mixing it with some sugar, in a little pot, the water being hot you must pour the *chocolate* therein.' He then suggested brewing it a score of times, pouring it back and forth between two pots to prevent it separating and then drank it straight down, ignoring the scum which had formed.

Coffee and chocolate are always described as being drunk from dishes until well into the eighteenth century, while tea is noted as being served in dishes and cups.

The early modern woman's diet was far more varied than might be supposed. A whole host of herbs and ingredients went into dishes, and a great deal of work was involved in preparing home-cooked food, usually via an open hearth. The physical effort of keeping a fire going at the right level and moving large pots made cooking a laborious task and one which all but the poorest housewife would have had a maid's help with. The suet pudding, both as a sweet and a savoury dish was very popular during this time, presumably as it was relatively straightforward to cook over a fire in a pot. Yet, convenience foods were already widely available in the towns and cities, with street traders selling everything from oysters to hot pies.

Many letters are filled with examples of food being exchanged between families. In October 1627 Brilliana Harley sent her husband a partridge pie with two peahens in it, and a runlet of mead from their home in Herefordshire; she also regularly sent down baskets of food for her son Ned at university. Another gentlewoman, Katherine Knyvett, sent her family in London some links of sausage and a pie which they 'were much pleased with.'

Then, as now, people lived on a mixture of home-made and shop-bought food, but in this era, how and what to feed the family, planning ahead to ensure that food was available during the bleak winter months and in times of hardship must have weighed heavily on women's minds.

Chapter Five

Women and Dress

Clothing is a key way in which we present ourselves to the world. Fashion has always meant different things to different ranks of people and, while someone at the top of the social scale like Elizabeth I owned some 3,000 dresses, the average woman living during her reign might have possessed one or two at most.

A satirical poem 'Mundus Muliebris or the Ladies Dressing Room' (1690), questionably attributed to Mary Evelyn (1665–1685), the daughter of the diarist John, comically exaggerated the needs of a young bride. However, it also offers a revealing guide to the clothing a gentlewoman in the late seventeenth century required in order to start her married life. The trousseau is extensive and includes:

A black silk gown,
an embroidered bodice,
4 long petticoats,
4 short petticoats,
3 manteaus [*cloaks*],
12 smocks,
12 smocks as nightdresses trimmed with Flanders lace,
2 waistcoats for mornings,
3 pairs of bodies (embroidered),
short under-petticoats,
shoes,
slippers,
knee-high stockings and garters,
ribbons,
3 fur muffs,
some ruffled decorative sleeves,

a quilted pocket,
velvet scarves,
white and black hoods and coifs,
a dozen pairs of gloves both fur-lined and lace trimmed ones,
a working apron from France
various items of jewellery.

The poem claims that it was but 'a poor miss' who could count the number of garments she owned. Despite the need for a dozen shifts or underskirts for daily changing, the wardrobe was based around a single silk dress, which could be made to appear very different, with the addition of various sleeves, petticoats and waistcoats. The dress would not be washed, as the undergarments would be, but instead sponged and brushed down, as required.

The basic dress of an early modern woman consisted of many layers. Everyone wore a linen shift or chemise next to their skin. Linen was worn next to the skin for its perceived ability to draw out dirt from the body and keep the wearer clean. A women's shift, or chemise, was like a long nightdress with triangular insets called gussets under the arms to allow free movement. The collar was usually squared, so the shift didn't show through the day dress. Many people wore the same shift day and night and would only remove it to swap for another on washday.

Next came the under-petticoats or kirtles, of which women might wear more than one, followed by the actual petticoat. This was often an ornate embroidered garment, designed to be visible through the slit in the front of the dress. From the mid-sixteenth century, a corset-like garment called a 'body' (which eventually became known as the bodice and, like underpants today, was referred to as a 'pair of bodys'). Stays, which later replaced the bodys and became a staple garment, were strengthened with baleen, a hard bone-line substance from the mouths of whales.

The body was worn over the underclothes and pulled in tight to create a firm, high chest and a narrow waist. Again, men and women both wore versions of this but the female one was particularly restrictive and limited movement – slouching while wearing a pair of bodys would be impossible. A hard wooden panel covered in fabric was placed at the centre of corset along the laced front, giving the stomach a taut, flat appearance. This was known as a busk or stomacher, and these often had highly elaborate embroidery as they showed through the lacings.

Women's clothing lacked sewn-in pockets but storage were provided by another garment, fashioned like a bag and worn on a belt around her waist underneath your petticoat. The 'pocket' acted like a small handbag, for storing money and essentials. Legs were covered by knitted knee-high socks or stockings, which were held up by garters or ribbons. Next came the dress, which was slipped over the head. Sleeves were added separately and tied on. A married woman would wear a chatelaine around her waist with her household keys and useful items, like scissors, attached, which was another mark of rank. In the winter both petticoats and sleeves might be quilted and padded for warmth.

In the mid-sixteenth century, as the corset was pulling the waist in, the skirt was growing bigger and bigger, with a farthingale or hooped petticoat worn under the dress to hold the skirt out. While the cut of the dress could be quite low, in some cases showing the majority of the breasts, most women would wear a lawn (a sheer fabric) scarf called a partlet around her chest, tucked into the dress to maintain her modesty. At the top of the partlet a frilly collar or 'ruff' was pinned, which is now considered synonymous with Elizabethan costume. A waistcoat or sleeveless long coat might then be added finally, with an apron worn to keep the dress clean, and a woollen cloak out of doors.

One thing notably absent from this list of early modern women's clothing was drawers or knickers, neither of which was worn in the seventeenth century. Indeed it is not until the nineteenth century, following the example of Queen Victoria that knickers became routinely worn in England. Many women wore cloths (clouts) to absorb their menstrual flow, which they would pin to their girdle. Elizabeth Pepys, the French-born wife of the diarist Samuel, was an exception, as she continued the French custom of wearing drawers, which was considered most unusual.

In May 1663 Pepys, who was jealous of Elizabeth's obvious enjoyment of the time she spent with her dancing master, stayed in bed late to watch his wife dress: 'I am ashamed to think what a course I did take by lying to see whether my wife did wear drawers to-day as she used to do [*usually does*], and other things to raise my suspicion of her, but I found no true cause of doing it.' Judging her behaviour by his own standards, Pepys wanted to check Elizabeth wore her customary underwear when having dancing lessons and so was not making intercourse easier by leaving them off.

The unusual nature of wearing drawers is borne out by a letter from Lady Mary Wortley Montagu who wrote from her continental travels to her sister in April 1717 that she had taken on the local fashions and 'the first part of my dress is a pair of drawers, very full that reach to my shoes, and conceal the legs more modestly than your petticoats. They are of a thin, rose-coloured damask, brocaded with silver flowers.'

Changing Fashions During the Early Modern Era

Although women's basic attire stayed the same, fashions did change during this period. Poet Mary Collier referred to this in a poem about her work as a washerwoman (as discussed in Chapter Two) and suggested that the early eighteenth century fashions would have seemed strange to earlier generations:

> *Cambricks and muslins, which our ladies wear,*
> *Laces and edgings, costly, fine, and rare,*
> *Which must be washed with utmost skill and care;*
> *With Holland shirts, ruffles and fringes too,*
> *Fashions which our fore-fathers never knew.*

In late Elizabethan times elite women finished off their outfits with elaborate gauze wings, so perhaps Colliers' forefathers wouldn't have been too shocked by the latest fashions in her day. Bodices and stomachers also grew longer during the later decades of Elizabeth I's reign, with the point of the stomacher reaching down to the pubic area. Into the early seventeenth century it became fashionable for women to wear puffed sleeves, slashed to let the colour-contrasting lining show through. Bodices then became shorter again, but ruffs grew larger and more elaborate. Ruffs disappeared by the end of the 1620s, as did the farthingale, and at the end of the seventeenth century, for a while the latest trend was to attach big bows to the front of a dress.

Fashions trickled down from London to the provinces at a much slower rate than nowadays and women in outlying areas would have worn clothes or ornaments that had been out of fashion in the city for decades. A good example of changing fashions is found in the letters of Sir Thomas Knyvett, who was in London in the House of Commons while his wife Katherine stayed on at their country house at Ashwellthorpe, in Norfolk. From her remote position, Katherine had to send to Thomas when she needed materials such as new bedding. On 26 November 1621 Thomas wrote to tell his wife that he had been looking for material as she requested but couldn't make a decision without her looking at some samples he was enclosing.

In June 1622 Thomas had been charged with getting Katherine a new dress made, but it seems he had not attended to his errand promptly. He wrote to tell her that 'your gown and things are making, but will not be done against Whit Sunday, which fault I must confess I deserve to be chidden for.' While Katherine was disappointed that her dress wouldn't be ready for the holiday, Thomas let her know in the same letter of a new Court style, which had all the 'great ladies' wearing plain white aprons. He also told his wife to pass on to a friend that the waistcoat she presumably had asked him to source was 'quite out of fashion.'

In the sixteenth century noblewomen wore long waistcoats, but by the end of the seventeenth these were shorter garments, associated with ordinary women and so shunned by the higher ranks. This didn't appear to bother Katherine, who still requested one the following year. Similarly, in 1623, Thomas sent his wife a piece of 'birdseye' for his aunt, who was staying with them, 'to make a ruff of.' This kind of lace would be spotted, as it seems to refer to all manner of spotted fabrics (Elizabeth Pepys in 1665 had a yellow silk birdseye hood, for example).

Crucially, as ruffs were going out of fashion Thomas told his wife to ensure that his aunt made hers small and loosely set, as this was the mode in the city now. In spring 1624 Thomas sent his wife a pair of silk stockings and some ribbons. He had taken an example of the type of white damask Katherine wanted a dress made from, but couldn't find any similar 'in all the town.' He asked her what she would have instead and reported that, 'all that I see worn is black, with rich petticoats and such ribbons as you have.' Sometimes Thomas' frustration with his missions shows through, as he apologised for the lace, saying he hoped it was suitable as he had 'no skill in buying lace' and that, try as he might, he had not been able to find any matching pearls for his aunt.

One fashion, which was probably peculiar to London in the early seventeenth century, was for women to wear men's clothes. Indeed, in 1620 John Chamberlain wrote a letter to the Bishop of London, claiming that King James had had enough of it. He demanded that the Bishop instruct the clergy to preach against this practice from their pulpits. According to Chamberlain, they were to 'inveigh vehemently and bitterly in their sermons against the insolency of our women, and their wearing of broad-brimmed hats, pointed doublets, their hair cut short or shorn, and some of them stilettos or poniards.' Stilettos were chunky daggers and poniards were the slimmer equivalent. No gentleman in the period would go out without his sword and it seems women were copying this too.

According to Chamberlain, James had added that, if this didn't stop the women, then he wouldn't hesitate to stop them by other means. How successful the King was is unclear, but he had been complaining about women filling up the court with enormous farthingales without success for years. In the later seventeenth century, actresses wearing men's clothes became part of the apparatus of theatre and seemed to go down well with audiences. The plays of Aphra Behn were famous for their breeched roles and Charles II's famous mistress, Nell Gwyn (1650–1687) specialised in these suggestive parts.

As Thomas Knyvett's correspondence with his wife above demonstrates, men and women seem to have been equally concerned about fashion and keeping up appearances. For example in December 1662 diarist Samuel Pepys felt ashamed that his wife Elizabeth did not have a new winter gown but had to go about in her taffeta one, when all other fashionable women had new mohair ones. Similarly Lancashire gentleman, Nicholas Blundell (1669–1737) considered it noteworthy in his diary that when his daughters were home from boarding school on the continent, he had to take them to be fitted for new body.

Hair: Curls, Coifs and Caps

Many portraits of seventeenth century women display the same hairstyle. Hair was curled into ringlets, with several smaller flatter curls arranged on the forehead, as a very short fringe. Hair was worn very high on the forehead, and women plucked their hairline to create an artificially high one. Towards the end of the seventeenth century, curled hair was worn piled on top of the head, with two ringlets or 'locks' left loose to fall down the front. One of these ringlets became the subject of Alexander Pope's famous poem, 'The Rape of the Lock' (1712), in which the Baron snips off one of Belinda's locks of hair at a party.

Married women wore their hair covered in a close fitting cap called a coif, which could have a veil attached. Hats were always worn outdoors, often at a jaunty angle, topped with feathers or pleated headdresses called *fontanges*. These remained in fashion throughout the century and Queen Mary II (1662–1694) was drawn wearing one in the 1690s. Puritans and other non-conformist sects had their own styles of dress, and the women in these groups often wore tall 'steeple' hats, which probably developed from the sixteenth century *copotain* tall hat fashionable in the 1590s. In the later seventeenth century hats were more like bonnets, tied under the chin with ribbons.

Shoes

Shoes were made by cordwainers, an occupation which had its own trade guild. They were available in different styles throughout the century, often consisting of a slip-on style with a rounded toe for the average woman, but could be very ornately decorated and high heeled for the wealthy or aristocratic woman. Everyday shoes would be made of leather, but higher-ranking ladies had delicate fabric shoes. They were often made to measure for those who could afford it, but also sold in set sizes, as one misogynistic poem, 'In Praise of his Mistresses' Beauty,' from a mid-seventeenth century anthology compiled by John Phillips, implies. The poet talks about his mistress being fat, with flea-bitten skin and:

Her pretty feet not 'bove fifteens,
So splayed as never was,
An excellent usher for a man
That walks the dewy grass.

Her feet were so large that if she walked ahead of a man, she would flatten the grass to save his feet from getting wet.

If shoes needed repairing they were taken to a cobbler. When women went out onto the streets, which were unpaved and often covered in unsavoury detritus, they would wear metal pattens or overshoes, which held them a couple of inches higher off the ground and stopped their shoes from being ruined, along with the hem of their dress. Agnes Beaumont (1652–1720) complained that after her father had thrown her out of his house, she had to walk home from church, 'ploshing through the dirt over my shoes,' because she had no pattens on.

Dressing According to Your Station

In their guide to running a godly household (1598), Robert Cleaver and John Dod proclaimed that the duties of a wife were: 'Firstly that she reverence her husband. Secondly, that she submit herself and be obedient unto him. And lastly that she do not wear gorgeous apparel, beyond her degree and place, but that her attire be comely and sober, according to her calling.'

This book seems to have been popular, as is it had run to nine editions by 1640. In early modern times, people judged your financial, social and even moral status by your clothing. More religiously-minded women wore plainer clothing to present themselves as pious to the outside world.

Wearing clothing that was considered appropriate to your station and rank in life was not merely a matter of propriety, but enshrined by law at the start of the period. Henry VIII formalised 'sumptuary laws,' declaring which groups of people could wear certain fabrics, furs and even colours, and, because she considered that the laws had been flouted too often, on 15 June 1574 Elizabeth I issued a declaration reminding people of their obligation and giving them 12 days to ensure that they were conforming.

The statute dictated that only those above the rank of Duchess could wear cloth of gold (fabric woven with gold thread), or sable fur; that only wives of Knights of the Garter or ladies of the bedchamber could wear red velvet, black fur, or lace made of gold or silver; only those of the rank of baroness or above were entitled to wear sequins or pearls sewn on to their partlets; those with an income of over a hundred pounds a year could wear damask or taffeta.

The list was essentially meant to make everyone's rank apparent at a glance. Not only were people expected to know their place in society, they had to ensure their appearance was in line with it too. Part of the reasoning behind the sumptuary rules was to protect British industry by allowing only those of the highest ranks to wear imported fabrics or furs. So, although at the start of the seventeenth century a woman could be fined or imprisoned for wearing or trying to buy a silk dress, when James I took office in 1603 he had the laws repealed as too restrictive. This would have had little impact on the average person, for whom London fashions would have seemed very remote.

Work Clothing: Servants and the Lower Classes

All aristocratic households issued their servants with a uniform, known as a livery; all the guilds such as bakers and apothecaries too, wore their own liveries (so they were also known as livery companies). The colour of ones clothes would make you instantly recognisable as an employee of a certain family or having a certain occupation. Female servants generally wore hand-me-down clothes from their mistresses, good quality but slightly dated garments.

For those lower down the social scale who were not in service, fashion was far less of a concern than keeping warm. Stays might be made of leather and be almost a once in a lifetime purchase. They would not be elaborate like those belonging to higher-ranking women and lacked a stomacher, instead being tightly laced up at the front. Their shifts, while similar to those of the higher ranks, were made out of courser fabric, such as home-spun hemp cloth. Clothes could be bought second-hand at rag fairs and were repaired and patched for as long as possible and then, when they were finally worn to rags, recycled as household cloths.

An anonymous late seventeenth century ballad describes a lane in London which sold exclusively second-hand clothes. 'The Humours of the Rag-Fair' describes how you could buy anything from frilly shirts to childbed linen from the second-hand tailors. The poem satirically notes that you could buy lovely knitted stockings, which were not above a quarter darned, and even second-hand shoes for five groats a pair (a groat was worth four old pennies, so 20 pence, but a new pair of basic shoes would cost around 2 shillings or 24 pence, highlighting the rip-off the poem thinks the second-hand fayre is).

A transaction in the record book of apothecary John Westover gives a useful guide to the price that ordinary people might have paid for new clothing. Westover ran a hospital along with his business, where he could keep patients who needed his attention close by, usually those suffering with mental illnesses. Elizabeth Jeanes resided there in 1688 with her brother paying for her board and lodge. Nathaniel Jeanes agreed to pay Westover 3 shillings and 6 pence for some new shoes and stockings (with the stockings being one shilling); he paid a further 3 shillings and 6 pence for a new pair of 'bodices,' with an additional farthing for the laces. (This account indicates that the language shift from 'bodys' to 'bodices' had happened by the late seventeenth century.) Nathaniel also paid out 8 shillings for his sister's linen and other necessaries, and 3 shillings and 4 pence for 4 yards of towelling.

Being thrifty was something that concerned the whole of this society, not just the poor. Lady Anne Clifford (1590–1676), for instance, noted in her diary that her husband had given her one of his old shirts to make into clouts. John Westover carefully noted even the few pennies he spent having Elizabeth Jeanes' coat mended and that he himself accepted a shoe repair (taping of his shoe) to the value of a shilling in part payment of a bill of 1 shilling and 6 pence for a fever tincture.

Clothing Worn on Special Occasions

Those of higher rank took to wearing black mourning clothing in the seventeenth century, but this was not a practice most could follow. Instead people tended to wear their soberest items of clothing when in mourning. Alternatively, a Royal procession or other spectacle would require lots of expensive, elaborate clothing for courtiers, for which there was no equivalent for ordinary people. Even Lady Elizabeth Delaval, who was the daughter of an Earl, ended up incurring serious debts for trying to keep up with the Court fashions while she worked there as a lady-in-waiting.

For their weddings women liked to have a new dress but this was not specifically a wedding dress. Samuel Pepys recorded with fondness his wife's new gold-trimmed petticoat on their wedding day. On other occasions such as New Year or Valentine's Day, people sometimes gave each other gifts of clothing, with gloves being a popular choice. People from the aristocratic Lady Anne Clifford to the middle-ranking Samuel Pepys gave gloves as gifts on such occasions.

While for most people clothing was home-made, passed down, and recycled until it fell to pieces, it is clear that with the rise of the middling sort, who made money from trade, that people enjoyed shopping for and buying clothes as much as other commodities. Clothing, however, was taken as representative of your character and means, and despite the repeal of the sumptuary laws people were still expected to dress according to their station in life.

Chapter Six

Personal Hygiene and Beauty

While it is certainly true that no era before our own has been as devoted to daily showers, or such a bewildering array of beauty products, it would be a mistake to assume that early modern women did not attend to their personal hygiene. Of course, ideas about cleanliness change from generation to generation. For example, a young man in the sixteenth century who had become sweaty through exertion would change his linen shirt to refresh himself rather than wash. It was a widely held belief that linen drew out and absorbed bodily impurities and so this made sense.

A small number of public bathing houses did exist in big cities such as London, but were advertised as places for therapeutic treatments and they were not places that ordinary men and women would go to clean themselves, not least since they carried an association with brothels or 'stews' with them, for good reason. Quack doctor, John Evans' 1696 advertisement for cures at his 'hummums' (or baths) in Brownlow Street, off Drury Lane, boasted that clients could take a sweat treatment in a hot bath, or a cold bath depending on their symptoms and also receive 'fine cupping' with reassuringly clean linen, for 3 shillings for one, or two for just 5 shillings.

While bath houses were more popular in Europe, at least until the repeated outbreaks of the plague discouraged people from using them, the association with immorality meant they were much rarer in England. Eighteen hot bath houses were licensed in London's Southwark district, on land owned by the Bishop of Winchester (the prostitutes who worked in the area were therefore known as 'Winchester Geese'). Royalty, of course, constituted the exception and Henry VIII had a tower with a bath and a toilet installed at Hampton Court Palace, following the European model, and when Elizabeth I took the crown she had access to baths with hot running water. This was beyond the comprehension of her average subject, for whom even running cold water was an unheard of luxury.

In addition to changing their clothes, people rubbed or brushed their skin with linen cloths to clean themselves. Individual body parts might be washed, normally with cold water. However, in the normal course of things, people tended to wash their hands and face regularly but were suspicious of washing other body parts too frequently.

Against the notions of common sense at this time, on the eve of her wedding, in December 1651 Yorkshire gentlewoman Alice Thornton decided to wash her feet. When she came down with a cold the next day, she wrote that she 'might have brought it upon myself by cold taken the night before, when I sat up late in preparing for the next day, and washing my feet at that time of year.' If she had washed her feet in the summer instead, she would have been less at risk of illness, for as physician John Pechey wrote in 1696, the washing of the feet and legs unseasonably, or at inappropriate times, could cause problems such as nose bleeds.

Dental Hygiene and Hair Removal

Several books of household management and even women's medical guides, such as *The Birth of Mankind,* offered hygiene and even beauty tips. *The Birth of Mankind* was an English translation of a European midwifery text book, first appearing in English in 1540 and dedicated to the short-lived Queen Catherine Howard (1523–1542). When a doctor called Thomas Raynalde reworked the book five years later for reissue, in addition to correcting some of the mistakes in the medical theories, he added a section on 'diverse beautifying recipes,' which encompassed personal hygiene treatments.

Topics covered in this section include cures for dandruff, and advice on depilation, or removing hair from 'places where it is unseemly,' which in this era included the forehead and temples. Most portraits from the period show women with artificially high hairlines, usually achieved by plucking with 'pincers' or tweezers, or a home-made, soap-based depilatory cream of arsenic and burnt limestone. It is likely that other bodily hair was removed in this way too. Being hairy was seen as undesirable because it was associated with a warmer, manly, highly-sexed body. Hannah Woolley's *The Accomplish'd Lady's Delight* (1675) advised women with body odour problems to pluck their armpit hair, and in early modern nude paintings body hair is seldom represented.

To clean teeth Raynalde recommended that, if they were very discoloured, readers should visit a barber to have them scoured clean. To keep up the effect, he advised daily cleaning between the teeth with a toothpick and rubbing them all over with the root of a mallow, or a powder made of ground pebbles. This advice sounds altogether more reliable than Woolley's recommendation, over a hundred years later, to make the teeth white and sound by taking 'a quart of Honey, and as much Vinegar, and half so much White-Wine, boil them together, and wash your Teeth therewith now and then.'

Dealing with Body Odours

The last two beauty treatments Raynalde offered were for people with 'stinking breath' and 'a rank savour of the armhole.' Halitosis was often caused by rotten teeth and so the cure was to go and have them 'plucked' out, otherwise a mouthwash made from clove and nutmeg would help sufferers. Woolley's cure for the same ailment was, she claimed, a proven one, although it required some commitment: 'Take two handfuls of cumin, and stamp it to powder, and boil it in wine, and drink the syrup thereof morning and evening for fifteen days, and it will help.'

Body odour was, Raynalde said, 'a vice' many people suffered from, which was 'loathsome.' As with all early modern medicine, the first place to look for a cure was in rebalancing the humours, as choleric or hotter bodied people, were thought to be more prone to this symptom. The treatment was a medicinal drink made from artichoke roots and white wine, which was intended to purge the body and remove the smell via the urine. Taken together with a regular change of linen, as was the standard method of keeping clean, according to Raynalde the problem should be solved.

Hannah Woolley's advice, mentioned above, also included white wine but as a wash not a drink. First, she said, you should pluck out the hairs, then wash the armpits in a wine and rose water mixture three or four times, and that would solve the problem. The advice for bad breath, dandruff, and smelly armpits detailed here was all given in *The Birth of Mankind*, the best-selling women's health guide of the day. The book reappeared in many forms and inspired spin-offs, including Woolley's popular household manual, repudiating the claim that people were unconcerned about their personal hygiene.

In addition to keeping herself clean and tidy by the standards of the day, it is clear the early modern woman was also interested in beauty treatments. Hannah Woolley's *Lady's Delight* has a section devoted to recipes describing how to make 'beautifying waters, oils, ointments, and powders, to adorn, and add loveliness to the Face and Body.'

Haircare

Women did not routinely wash their hair, but mainly combed it through with a fine tooth comb a couple of times a day, removing the dead skin cells and excess oils, keeping the hair remarkably clean. It was then kept sweet-smelling by the use of various liniments or creams made from herbs such as lavender and cloves. As a proverb in John Ray's 1670 collection noted, the normal practice was to 'wash your hands often, your feet seldom, and your head never.'

If you did decide to wash your head (as hair washing was usually referred to), then it was imperative that you dried it thoroughly before you risked catching a cold. Thomas Raynalde advised covering the head with warm cloths after washing, but he also warned that you should only wash your hair in the morning before eating, an hour before supper, or at least five hours after having supper. Raynalde was unusual in being an advocate for washing the hair, providing you took the precautions he outlined, as by doing so you might 'purify the skin of the head, and steadfast the hair from falling, levitate [*relieve*] and lighten the head with all the senses therein contained, and greatly comfort the brains.'

How many women took this advice is a moot point; diarist John Evelyn famously described the benefits of the annual summer hair wash he undertook each year, using warm water and sweet herbs, in a way that suggests it was thought unusual. He claimed to find it most refreshing, and the results he obtained were much like those promised by Raynalde: his whole head was refreshed, and he claimed that his hair stayed bright and clean for the rest of the year.

One time when it was usual for women to wash their hair was if it was losing its colour, when a good wash in lye soap seems to have been in order, removing the build-up of grease would certainly make the hair seem brighter. Otherwise, to blacken the hair, a comb dipped in black leading could be used (this was also recommended for men's beards). Felix Platter's *Golden Practice of Physick* (1664, translated into English by Nicholas Culpeper) warned that you shouldn't over darken your hair, as that was unattractive, and that if it was naturally very black, then you could lighten it by washing it with lye soap and then use the smoke from burning sulphur, known as brimstone. Platter advised that hair could be reddened with the juice of radishes or made blond with washes made from ingredients such as alum. Although William Langhan's herbal from 1597 advised the use of boiled thyme (epithime) as a gentler alternative to 'yellow' the hair.

Black hair definitely seems to have been out of favour, as Raynalde even suggested that people with black hair were much more prone to dandruff than any other hair colours, though it was surely just more visible in dark hair. Red hair too was thought undesirable. The author of *The Ladies Dictionary* (1694), indeed wrote that, 'As for the colour of the Hair, opinions are various [...] but above all that it be not red.' Medium brown seems to have been considered the ideal colour.

As well as recipes to lighten the hair, Hannah Woolley gave recipes to stop hair falling out, which included a soap made from burnt pigeon dung. This was used too for restoring hair that had stopped growing from over-plucking, useful in an era in which an artificially high, plucked hair line was thought desirable. Woolley also advised washing hair with lye soap mixed with the ashes of burned frogs or goat dung to make it grow thick.

Facial Care

Most of the beauty recipes given in health and household manuals are concerned with enhancing a woman's natural beauty, not falsely altering her appearance. So for example, Woolley's advice for chapped lips was to, 'Rub them with the Sweat behind your Ears, and this will make them smooth, and well coloured,' and similarly finger nails could be encouraged to grow with an application of honey and wheatgrass.

A natural pale complexion with a subtle blush to the cheek was the ideal, so cures were offered to remove freckles, for which Woolley advised using almond oil or hare's blood, and removing too much redness from the complexion with a jelly made from various pulses. Significantly, many beauty guides also offered potions to repair the damage caused to a woman's face by the ravages of smallpox, a prevalent disease at this time. Smallpox was endemic in the early modern period and often left its victims horribly scarred. Lady Katherine Howard, Countess of Suffolk (1564–1638), was struck down by this in 1619. The disease marked the end of an awful year in which her family's influence at Court ended dramatically. Her daughter, Lady Frances Howard Countess of Somerset had been imprisoned in the Tower of London for murder, and she herself had spent ten days in the Tower charged with bribery. The pox then ruined the beauty that Katherine had used to enhance her wealth and influence. Lady Katherine went on to live until the age of 74 in retirement in Essex, but never tried to reclaim her position at Court.

The scourge of this disease was to come to an end in the eighteenth century largely through the actions of Lady Mary Wortley Montagu who introduced the inoculation practices she had seen on the Continent into England. Here a piece of thread was dipped in an infected pustule and placed in a small cut on the healthy person's body. Wortley Montagu was so impressed with this that she had her own children inoculated in a practice others copied.

Cures for the marks this disease left behind were many and various, but Woolley said that the best one she had come across was 'to wash the Face one day with the Distilled water of strong Vinegar, and the next day with the water wherein Bran and Mallows have been boiled; and continue this twenty days, or a Month together.'

Make-up

While making the most of your natural beauty was considered to be a proper thing to do, enhancing your face with make-up wasn't something that the average woman would have considered appropriate in early modern England. When people sang about 'Betty Carey's lips and eyes / make all hearts their sacrifice,' they were referring to her natural features. Elizabeth 'Betty' Carey

(1632/3–1679) married John, Viscount Mordaunt in 1656 and left a deeply spiritual diary, so she is now remembered for her piety not her beauty.

The Bible warned women against wearing make-up; Timothy 2.9, for example, warned women not to braid their hair or wear excessive ornamentation. Polemics taking this literally, such as preacher Thomas Tuke's *A Discourse Against Painting and Tincturing of Women* (1616) were often printed. This short collection of anti–make-up verse opens with a poem by Arthur Dowton:

> *A loam* [clay] *wall and painted face are one;*
> *For th'beauty of them both is quickly gone.*
> *When the loam is fallen off, then lathes appear,*
> *So wrinkles in that face from th'eye to th'ear.*
> *The chastest of your sex condemn these arts,*
> *And many that use them, have rid* [ridden] *in carts.*

This slightly hysterical poem makes a link between make-up and criminality, including prostitution, implying that the sort of woman who wears it will end her days riding in a cart to the gallows.

This was just one side of the story and the women of the court, of course, lived by different rules, as is evidenced by Queen Elizabeth's white leaded face. Just as there were books fulminating against make-up, so there were books detailing methods of making cosmetics. In 1658 a translation of a popular continental book, *Natural Magic* by Giambattista della Porta, appeared and it included a section entitled, 'How to adorn Women, and make them Beautiful.' This book is just as misogynistic as the texts railing against make-up, as it is founded on the premise that women should wear make-up to avoid offending their husbands.

The author described what he claimed were safer recipes for whitening the skin than the traditional concoctions made from mercury, which rotted the skin and teeth, but ironically these were made from the equally harmful ceruse or lead. The author then included tips directed at men to help them discover whether a woman they are conversing with has a painted face or not. Della Porta recommended chewing saffron and then breathing on the woman, which would, he said, turn the make-up yellow, but leave her skin entirely unaffected if natural.

The satirical poem attributed to Mary Evelyn, 'Mundus Muliebris or the Ladies Dressing Room' (1690) describes a young woman's dressing table paraphernalia and products. It was strewn with washes, unguents and cosmetics, brushes for her gowns and hair and bejewelled bodkins for pinning up her hair. Because of the time she would spend in dressing, the table also contained tea and chocolate pots and dishes of sweets. The subject had some chicken skin gloves to wear in bed, putting them on after applying hand–cream to keep her skin soft.

When this poem was published appended to it was a recipe for 'puppidog water,' which was used as a beauty treatment to clarify the skin. This was once thought to refer to puppy urine; however, the recipe for puppy water describes a far more sinister process of taking a nine-day-old puppy, killing it, then roasting it until cooked, and discarding the guts. The remains were then put in a still with two quarts of Canary sack (dry Spanish wine), some butter, snail shells and distilled. Then the remains were to be dripped through a sugar loaf. In March 1664, Samuel Pepys declared himself discontented when he found that his wife had bought some puppy-water, on the advice of his Aunt Wight who, he said, rather ungraciously had asked Elizabeth to get her some for 'her ugly face' without his uncle's knowledge.

Like all things though, fashions in beauty products changed, and in the eighteenth century physician John Maubray noted a worrying trend of women using make-up to make themselves look green and ill, in imitation of the disease of greensickness (chlorosis). In *The Female Physician* (1724) Maubray wrote that: 'I have known many women, in France, and Germany, who have been so far from thinking it an ugly colour, that they have esteemed it beautiful; and have used very pernicious things to gain an appropriate colour to themselves.' This was a recognised fashion in England as well as in Europe, and recipes for making the face appear green-tinged are given in books such as *Natural Magic*. This was part of an attempt by young women to seem grown-up. Pale, green-sick women were thought attractive and so by appearing pale, the girl showed herself to be sexually mature.

One fashion in facial adornment which came into England in the mid-seventeenth century was the facial patch, known as black patches or spots. These were small pieces of black fabric or leather cut into shapes such as stars or crescent moons and stuck on the face, often used to cover a smallpox scar or similar imperfection. Such was their appeal that women wanted to wear them as fashion accessories even when they had nothing to cover.

Elizabeth Pepys bought some patches, but it took some persuasion to get her husband to let her go out in public wearing them. In a diary entry for 4 November 1660, Pepys recorded: 'My wife seemed very pretty to-day, it being the first time I had given her leave to wear a black patch.' People who saw make-up as sinful inevitably saw patches in the same light, with one 1662 poem, by Rowland Watkyns, describing how, 'The creature strives the creator to disgrace, / By patching that which is a perfect face.'

As well as patches mouse hide could be fashioned into false eyebrows. A poem from 1719, 'A Beautiful Young Nymph going to Bed,' by satirist Jonathan Swift (1667–1745), describes an old prostitute sticking on her mouse hide eyebrows in an attempt to look younger, as well as using wadding to plump out her cheeks to make her look more youthful.

For seventeenth century noblewoman and author Margaret Cavendish, Countess of Newcastle, make-up and beauty regimes were defined by social rank. In *Sociable Letters* (1664), she wrote that:

> *country Housewives take more pleasure in milking their cows, making their butter and cheese, and feeding their poultry, than great ladies do in painting, curling* [their hair], *and adorning themselves, also they have more quiet &*
> *peaceable minds and thoughts, for they never, or seldom, look in a glass to view their faces, they regard not their complexions, nor observe their decays.*

However, writing a decade earlier in *The World's Olio* (1655), Margaret had previously launched into a spirited defence of 'painting,' arguing that clothes are just as unnatural but no one advocated walking around naked. What is clear in all the polemic and argument though, is that housewives all over the country might have experimented with recipes to moisturise and keep their skin comfortable and healthy, but for the majority of Englishwomen the idea of face paint would never be acceptable.

Part III

Women and Reproduction

Chapter Seven

Menstruation:
The Time of the Month

For the majority of women today, menstruation is a normal, more or less regular part of everyday life. Being aware of how their cycle affects their mood or having methods in place to deal with painful cramps just constitute part of life. This chapter examines how far this was true for women in early modern England.

Whilst the physical experience of a monthly bleed was no different, the way it was understood, written and talked about, and managed was certainly very different from today. It has been argued that women in past times had fewer periods, because they were either perpetually pregnant or lactating, if not too malnourished to menstruate. While it is true that in times of food shortage such as in the famines of the 1590s or in a harsh winter, poorer women might not have had their periods, most women would expect many years of menstrual cycles.

The average age given in medical books for menarche or a first period was between 12 and 14, and the average age of marriage in the seventeenth century was around 26, which immediately suggests the possibility of at least a decade of uninterrupted cycles. Secondly, the average marriage produced between five and seven births, fewer than many suppose. The age that most medical texts stated that women could expect to experience the menopause was from 49 onwards.

Yet, the exceptions to these rules were aristocratic women, who might be placed in arranged marriages in their teens and then go on to produce a baby every 18 months or so. However, this was not the experience of women further down the social scale, for whom marriage came much later in life. For the majority of women, their experiences and expectations of the way their reproductive bodies might work are not so different from our own.

Medical Explanations for Menstruation

Writing about menstruation, ancient Greek physician Galen said that it was necessary for women to bleed each month because they led sedentary lives, and so built up an excess of blood, one of the four bodily humours. This didn't happen to men, Galen explained, because they worked harder and more physically than women and so sweated out their excess humours.

In the early modern period, Helkiah Crooke (1576–1648), the author of a popular medical textbook in print from 1615, *Mikrokosmographia; or a Description of the Body of Man*, explained this theory by describing how women spent their days sitting and embroidering (or 'pricking on a clout'). He claimed that due to this, throughout the month, excess blood built up until it was discharged as a menstrual period. It didn't happen in very young girls because their excess blood was used up in growing, so the reason why they began menstruating at 14 was that they had stopped growing. This explanation for menstruation was known as the 'plethora theory' and was the most common explanation for women's periods at the time.

Great importance was placed on evacuations in humoral medicine. Physicians regularly prescribed purging medicines to make their patients sick (vomits) or go to the toilet (enemas) and then gleefully recorded how many times a patient had been to 'stool' after a treatment. This was because evacuation in all forms was thought to be one of the environmental or 'non-natural' factors in maintaining health as discussed in Chapter 4. The six non-natural factors were six key elements imagined to affect bodily functions: air, sleep, intake, evacuations, movement, and emotions. In this context, then, it is easy to see why regular periods were seen as so essential to women's health by early modern doctors.

The emphasis placed on regular evacuations also explains why a missed menstrual period was not necessarily taken as an indication of potential pregnancy – rather it might just indicate that something had gone awry with the woman's humoral balance. Indeed, a missed period was often given way down the list of indicators of pregnancy. For example, midwife Jane Sharp who published *The Midwives Book* (1671) drawing on her 30 years of personal experience, gave 14 signs of pregnancy; missed periods are sixth in her list, after symptoms such as 'sour belching.'

There were two other theories put forward to explain why women had periods and they were known as the ferment and lunar theories. The latter, quite straightforwardly, held that the action of the moon caused women to bleed on a monthly basis but, while this theory was being advocated in print as late as the 1970s, early modern doctors regularly contended that it was flawed and easily dismissed. If the moon caused periods, they argued, then every woman of menstruating age would have a period at the same time. However, most medics did think that the moon had some influence on women's cycles and that younger women were more likely to bleed at the rising moon and older ones as the moon waned.

The other theory, the ferment, was only fashionable for a few decades. It held that, much as in the fermenting of alcohol, somewhere in the female body a ferment brewed until it reached a critical point and then bleeding broke out, with the process beginning again every month. The site where this might have happened was never found, although one doctor, James Drake (1667–1707) claimed that this was what the gallbladder was for. Since there was no empirical evidence to support it, this theory died out by the middle of the eighteenth century.

Whereas now menstruation is understood as the loss of the womb–lining, blood and other matter, in the past menstruation was presumed to be made up of blood lost from the veins of the womb. The reason that pregnant women didn't have periods, some early modern doctors speculated, was because the foetus fed on menstrual blood. In the first few months of a pregnancy some women still experience menstrual bleeding, which now might be explained in terms including a threatened miscarriage, but then this was conceived as happening because a tiny, developing foetus didn't need all the blood a woman lost in a period, so she still bled the excess out.

Humoral medicine was concerned with keeping the fluids within the body in balance. The need to keep up a regular menstrual cycle was seen as so important that of the over 300 plants listed in Nicholas Culpeper's *Complete Herbal* (1655), around a third were used to provoke menstruation. Another one of the main methods for bringing on a period was to let blood from the ankle, which was thought to encourage the blood to flow down the body.

Of course, the widespread medical concern to keep women's periods regular also makes it possible that a woman could use this excuse to obtain a covert abortion. Jane Sharp was clearly aware of this possibility when she warned that to give medicine to bring on a period in a woman who might be pregnant constituted murder.

There were a bewildering number of, often strange, alternative names for menstruation. Some of these were an attempt to euphemistically describe the event to avoid referring to it directly, but others were just the names people used for it. The most popular was 'flowers,' or 'the flowers,' which might appear in sentences such as 'she has her flowers upon her,' for example. In the seventeenth century some dictionaries and medical writers claimed that this word was a corruption of the Latin *fluor* or flow, but in fact the name is a very old one, used all across Europe and originating in horticulture. As Jane Sharp explained, it was used because 'fruit follows,' flowers, which is to say, that women who never had periods couldn't conceive.

After flowers, the next most popular names were 'courses' or 'terms,' which both derive from the regularity of periods, in the natural course of things. Doctors, on the other hand, just as they do now, often preferred to use Latin names and so referred to periods as the *menses*. In the later seventeenth and into the eighteenth century, the shift in medicine to Greek from Latin saw doctors use the word *catamenia* instead, as this is the Greek for 'monthly.' The most common modern name for menstruation, 'periods,' has its roots in the early modern era, when doctors would refer to the menstrual period, which is to say the period of time when a woman might be expected to menstruate. Over time this became shortened to 'period.'

Other phrases were more euphemistic, and women might have referred to themselves as being 'unwell' or having the 'monthly sickness.' These euphemisms survived well into the twentieth century, of course. Phrases such as 'gift of nature' or the biblical 'time common to women' were sometimes used too. The name menstruation itself, which nowadays is the formal term, also originated in the seventeenth century. The first example of its use that I have been able to find is from 1686, when Gideon Harvey (1636–1702), in *The Conclave of Physicians*, presented an argument between physicians about whether a woman with menstrual problems should be prescribed a cordial or not, and said that he was referring to a case of menstruation.

Theories Surrounding Menstrual Blood

As far back as the seventh volume of Pliny the Elder's *Natural History*, in the first century BCE, ideas about the magical, and even evil powers of menstrual blood and menstruating women have appeared in print. Pliny claimed that menstrual blood was so potent that just the touch of a menstruating woman could result in all sorts of mayhem from causing wine to go sour, trees and crops to die, dogs to go mad upon tasting it, and mirrors to become cloudy after being looked into by a menstruating woman, and the air to be filled with a horrible stench.

He continued: 'it is certain that when their hives are touched by women in this state bees fly away, at their touch linen they are boiling turns black, the edge of razors is blunted, brass contracts copper rust and a foul smell, especially if the moon is waning at the time, mares in foal if touched miscarry, nay the mere sight at however great a distance is enough.'

These ideas were reprinted in early modern medical books and even appear in gardening manuals. These texts took the theory that menstruating women posed a threat to others seriously, as well they might, since many medical books of the time also advised that having sex with a woman having her period would make a man's penis become cancerous or even leprous.

Not everyone held with these outlandish views, however. As early as 1545, Thomas Raynalde declared that he would not waste his paper and ink in the reproduction of what he denounced as 'shameful lies and slander' about the 'venomous and dangerous infective nature of the woman's flowers or terms [*periods*], which all be but dreams and plain dotage.' Raynalde argued that this blood could not be venomous or nature wouldn't have decided that it should be used to nourish 'tender and delicate infants,' both in the womb and in the form of breast milk.

Of course, Raynalde's rebuttal, even though it was laid out in the most popular medical guide of the time, didn't stop these beliefs being regularly reproduced as fact. Jane Sharp took pains to explain that, while the blood itself was pure, if the woman was ill her period would be used as a conduit to purge other bad humours from her body, thus making it seem like the blood was to blame.

Another clue to what women themselves might have thought of these amazing stories can be seen in James Drakes' 1707 medical book, in which he declared that he was only mentioning these myths in order to deny them and to show up the eminent doctors or 'men of great authority, who have been prevailed upon to believe what women at all times would laugh at.' While women might have laughed at the myths, nevertheless authoritative texts continued to reproduce them and so they must have influenced society's views to some extent.

Clouts and Rags: Sanitary Protection

Some early modern women would have routinely used folded cloths to absorb their menstrual flow, which were known as 'clouts' or 'rags.' Pieces of cloth used in a variety of household chores were generally referred to as clouts and were usually made from old cloth, often linen, cut to size, sometimes hemmed, and then employed as dishcloths, bandages, or in sanitary uses such toilet rags. Paper was not routinely used for this purpose, as it was too expensive, and unlike rags could not be reused.

The choice of linen as the material for most medical and sanitary purposes resulted from the belief that clean linen could draw off moisture from the body. Clouts used for sanitary protection were undoubtedly folded over and it is possible that flour was also added between the layers to aid their absorbency. Folded cloths were called the double clout, as can be seen in an abusive verse aimed at the actress Eleanor (Nell) Gwyn, the well-known mistress of Charles II. The verse claimed that Nell was 'famed for not wearing of the double clout: Her flowers of late have left their wonted source and through her mouth have taken another course,' which is to say that she no longer menstruated because her 'corruption,' as her detractors called her periods, flowed from her mouth instead, through speaking of her political alignment to the Stuart court.

The double clout would be fastened to a girdle, which was a belt worn around the waist – a necessary precaution in an age before underwear. For many poorer women though, even rudimentary sanitary protection in the form of clouts was beyond their means and they routinely bled into their shifts.

Internal sanitary protection was not normally used in this era, mainly because it was thought medically unsafe to hinder the blood flow. The exception to this rule might have been prostitutes. A poem written by Restoration courtier John Wilmot, the Earl of Rochester (1647–1680) alludes to this as a possibility. Rochester's poem, 'Song' ('By all loves soft, yet mighty Powers'), describes the experience of sleeping with a prostitute during her period.

The lyric is meant to be shocking, since it was passed around his peer group in manuscript and was published abroad after his death. The titillation factor is high, not least because sexual intercourse during a period was forbidden by the Church. Rochester advised men not to 'fuck in times of flowers,' not merely because of the religious taboo, but rather for aesthetic reasons:

> *Fair nasty nymph, be clean and kind,*
> *And all my joys restore;*
> *By using Paper still* [always] *behind,*
> *And sponges for before.*

Ordinary women had to choose between bleeding into their undergarments, or fashioning a clout from old linen, if they had access to it. Higher-ranking women would undoubtedly have used clouts fastened to their girdles.

Period Pain and Heavy Bleeding

For many women periods are associated with pain and discomfort. This pain was not associated in the early modern period with the contracting of the womb, as it is nowadays, but instead was assumed to be the result of the veins stretching while discharging the blood into the uterus. The pain was then envisaged as coming from blood, which was thickened by corrupt material the body was trying to expel. The types of analgesia or pain relief available to early modern women reflect the fact that their pain was linked with a need to expel tainted matter.

Crooke's *Mikrokosmographia* (1615) described the effect of menstrual cramps on the sufferer in a chapter detailing the sympathy between the uterus and the other major organs of the female body:

Between the Kidneys and the womb the consent is evident in the torments and pains in the Loins which women and maids have in or about the time of their courses [periods]. *In so much as some have told me they had as least bear a child as endure that pain; and myself have seen some to my thinking by their deportment; in as great extremity in the one as in the other.*

While a 1664 version of Nicholas Culpeper's translation of Daniel Sennert's *Book of Practical Physick* commented that periods 'must flow without any great Symptom,' it was known that some women suffered from terrible pain, which Crooke described as the equivalent of labour pains. Normally medical books recommended that pain could be treated with 'attenuating' herbs to steady the flow, or laudanum-based medications made from a mixture of alcohol and opiates, which would ease the pain.

The main treatment for women who experienced heavy bleeding, or 'flooding' was the same as those recommended for period pain. The first treatment would consist of medicines to narrow the blood vessels. Other purgative treatments, such as laxatives might be prescribed, in the belief that the body was attempting to rid itself of other waste and using the menstrual blood to carry it away. Alternatively, blood-letting might have been used in the days just before the expected period, to draw off the excess.

Brilliana, Lady Harley of Brampton Bryan seems to have suffered from excessive bleeding during her periods and it seems that she had received a letter from her son Ned, who was studying at Oxford University, urging her to see her doctor about it. Brilliana answered saying:

I thank you, my dear Ned, for wishing I should take something of him [her doctor]*; but my illness comes at certain times, and without I should send for him just at that time, I cannot have him then to give me anything: for he would have me take something and be let blood two or three days before I am ill, as I used to be.*

As she said, it would have been difficult for women to work out exactly when two or three days before their period would be and therefore know when it was appropriate to call the doctor. There was no knowledge of ovulation until the nineteenth century and so the exact reason for the cyclical nature of menstruation remained a mystery. Brilliana did compromise though, and agreed that should she be taken ill next time her son was home, then she would let him call for the doctor.

Absent or Irregular Periods

Periods and their regularity were seen as vital to women's health. As Jane Sharp wrote, periods were tricky to keep in balance, as they:

> *sometimes flow too soon, sometimes too late, they are too many or too few, or are quite stopt that they flow not at all. Sometimes they fall by drops, and again sometimes they overflow; sometimes they cause pain, sometimes they are of an evil colour and not according to nature; sometimes they are voided not by the womb but some other way; sometimes strange things are sent forth by the womb.*

Given the contemporary humoral understanding of the body, the amount of print devoted to how to keep periods in balance was justified. Frustratingly, we have very few records created by women themselves describing how they felt about their periods. Most accounts come from medical men, although they do sometimes record consultations and report a woman's concerns, often noting her woman's reluctance to tell him the problem.

Even when elite women wrote to one another about their periods, they referred to them in the most oblique ways, for instance implying that they might be pregnant because they have not received any 'visits.' This lack of evidence gives a sense that women were reluctant to talk openly about such matters, which is strange in a culture that openly discussed bowel movements. It suggests that the sense of shame periods evoked – which stems back to Eve's sin in the Bible, along with the myths about the poisonous and almost magical qualities of this blood – meant that women got on with their periods as privately as possible and were disinclined to discuss them in writing at least.

Chapter Eight

Pregnancy:
Being Big with Child

After an early modern couple were married, the normal assumption was that children would soon follow. However, this wasn't always quite so straightforward in practice. Marriage was promoted as the ideal state after the Reformation, but in the highly religious atmosphere of early modern England the Church provided detailed guidance about exactly when and how a married couple were allowed to make love.

For example, sex was forbidden if a woman was having her period, firstly it was deemed a sin, as the woman was considered unclean – and indeed this was picked up on in medical texts which suggested that a man's penis could become infected or the skin might even be scorched off through penetrating a menstruating woman. This theory is what William Whately was referring to in his 1617 guide to marriage *The Bride-Bush*, when he stated that married couples' 'nuptial meetings must be seasonal' and that anything less was simply unlawful. Whately even advised young wives not to be embarrassed to tell their husbands that they were having a period, because otherwise they were letting their husbands commit a mortal sin.

The second reason that sex was banned during menstruation was that it was believed that if a child was conceived during this forbidden time, then it might be deformed in some way. This belief was so common that, on the eve of his son's wedding, diarist John Evelyn wrote to warn him that not only should this be avoided because it was indecent, but it would also leave any resultant child 'disposed to leprosy, & marks the children with evident signs of the parents' incontinency.' These marks were imagined to be visible, through diseases such as leprosy or birthmarks often called strawberry or port-wine birthmarks, or even red hair, for example.

Other occasions when sex was forbidden included religious holy days, namely Fridays and Sundays, and fast days. Fast days were called by both the government and the Church as a day of abstinence and reflection at times of national crisis. A proclamation was issued on 6 July 1665, stating that the first Wednesday of each month should be kept as a public day of fasting, to atone for God's displeasure, which had manifested as a plague outbreak. Fasting involved abstaining from food and drink, but sex and other pleasures were forbidden as well.

How far people followed all these rules is impossible to say, but there are plenty of examples in diaries of couples expecting a new baby while the mother was still nursing an older child, a practice which was similarly frowned upon in medical texts. Essex vicar Isaac Archer (1641–1700) noted in his diary that his wife was obliged to stop nursing one of their infants when she realised she was pregnant again. On 20 March 1647 Jane Josselin told her husband that she was sure she was seven weeks pregnant with a boy. On 9 May she decided to wean her toddler Jane, who was then about 18 months old. In fact, Jane Josselin's next child wasn't born until 11 February 1648, suggesting that she became pregnant sometime later than she had initially supposed. The child was a boy, though.

Sex while breastfeeding was not recommended, since it was thought that a new pregnancy would take the nourishment away from the nursling and weaken them. The number of cases of pregnancy while women were still nursing shows that couples did not stick to this particular prohibition, even if they observed other rules to lesser or greater degrees.

Alice Thornton, who seems to have favoured her son Robert, whom she called Robin, recorded how she breastfed him until two weeks before the birth of her next child Joyce. This is an extraordinary thing to admit in the context in which she was writing, given that the milk of a pregnant woman was to be harmful for the nursling, and, indeed, Alice herself removed her daughter Betty from her wet-nurse, Daphne Lightfoot's home when Daphne became pregnant.

It is remarkable that people had sex at all, considering the lack of privacy in the early modern bedroom. If a family employed servants then they might well sleep on pull out truckle beds at the foot or side of the marital bed, and the only privacy couples could rely on was afforded by the curtains around the bed.

Conceiving a Child

Whenever conception occurred, this was seen as due to God's benevolence towards the couple. Medically, it was explained to have happened in two ways. The first model was inherited from Aristotle and reasoned that a woman's womb was like a fertile field in which the husband's sperm implanted a whole baby, leaving the woman's role as purely the carrying of the baby to term. This meant that sometimes conception was referred to in terms of the agent and the patient, with the man as the agent of conception and the woman the passive patient.

The second, more common model came down from Galen and dictated that both partners needed to reach orgasm to produce seed which joined together to make a baby. This model encouraged husbands to ensure their wives were sexually satisfied to conceive and so medical books would describe the appropriate amount of 'lascivious tickling' or foreplay necessary for women to climax.

There was another consequence of this theory, however, that a pregnancy, in law, ruled out the possibility that the child could have been conceived through rape. It was widely believed that if the woman did not enjoy sex then she would be unable to conceive, as she would not release seed. Jane Sharp saw that this wasn't necessarily true and so modified the sentiment found in her sources to write that couples must be nice to one another, as 'extreme hatred is the reason why women seldom or never conceive when they are ravished.' The term 'seldom' was a considerable shift from the received wisdom of 'never' often posited in similar books.

If a couple was struggling to conceive then the medical books had plenty of suggestions for them to try. Sometimes infertility was recognised to be of a type that was incurable and Jane Sharp cautioned that sometimes infertility signalled that the marriage was unlawful; marriage was for procreation and if a person had married knowing themselves to be infertile, because of some deformity for example, then the marriage was void.

Strictly speaking, this would mean that the Hickmans, a couple living in Stafford during the 1730s, had an unlawful marriage. Mrs Hickman was visited by her doctor, Richard Wilkes (1691–1760), because she was not having periods, despite apparently being well in other respects. Wilkes found that Mrs Hickman had a fused hymen, or no opening to her vagina from which blood could flow. Understandably, she was unwilling to undergo surgery to correct this, not simply due to the risks and pain involved, but because as Wilkes noted, 'she and her husband were content, and therefore she was not willing to undergo that operation. She is now about 30 years of age, strong, hearty and full of flesh.'

Cases such as this cast doubt on the premise that people adhered to every piece of religious law; despite the fact that this couple had no chance of a family, they were a happy couple. Other cases of infertility were ascribed to the couple being unsuited due to their conflicting humours, and this was one of the reasons against young women being married to very elderly men.

Despite the assumptions made at the court of Henry VIII, when he was struggling to beget a male heir, there was no automatic presumption that the fertility problems always lay with the woman. As the doctor and medical author Thomas Raynalde (who used the Aristotelian model of woman as a field, albeit one which lovingly nourished and embraced the foetus) wrote in his 1545 reproduction guide, there were three parts to a successful conception: the seed, the sower, and the earth. If, Raynalde wrote, 'there be fault in any of these three, then shall there never be due generation, unto such time as the fault be removed or amended.'

Luckily, Raynalde knew of a test to see whether the fault lay with the man or the woman. The method was to soak wheat and barley grains in each party's urine for 24 hours and then plant the seeds in pots. Keep watering the pots with the respective urine for the next couple of weeks and see which one grew into a plant. However, Raynalde himself said that the plan was a little far-fetched and unlikely to be much use.

A more reliable test, which he claimed came down from Hippocratic writing, involved using a fume. This meant putting the smoke from a fragrant substance like musk or amber underneath a woman's skirts and if the scent rose up through her body to her nose, then she was open enough to conceive and the fault did not lie with her.

For Raynalde, any fault with a woman's fertility was naturally based on the humoral model; if the womb was too wet, too dry, too hot, or too cold, he wrote, then it could not support a pregnancy. Each of these characteristics was linked to a humour, so cold went with melancholy, dry with choler, hot with sanguine, and moist with phlegmatic. Adjusting and rebalancing the humours of the woman, he explained would solve her infertility.

Pregnancy Tests

To know for certain whether a woman had conceived was difficult until reliable testing was invented during the twentieth century. Thomas Raynalde suggested that the main signs of pregnancy were: lighter periods, which eventually stopped; rounder and harder breasts; cravings; thicker urine; a feeling that the womb had closed up.

Pregnancy cravings were well recorded. In fact, among the signs of pregnancy that Jane Sharp gave was an unnatural desire to eat or drink inappropriate things, from unripe fruit to candles, cloth, sand, coal or ash, tobacco pipes, soil, and even stone. This was well documented, and Sharp includes a story, also given in several other medical books, which tells how some women 'with child have longed to bite off a piece of their husband's buttocks.'

Jane Sharp's list of the signs of pregnancy started with a tendency to tremble or shiver, which she claimed was caused by the body's heat being drawn down to the womb to support the conception. She also claimed that this process would make the stomach appear flatter than normal, as the womb sank down to 'cherish' the conception. Sharp also mentions mood swings, whereby the pregnant woman 'will be merry, or sad suddenly upon no manifest cause.' As discussed in the previous chapter, a missed period only made it on to point six of Jane Sharp's list of the signs of pregnancy, after 'sour belching,' since it was taken primarily as a sign that a woman's humours were out of balance rather than of possible conception.

For non-medical men and women though, a missed period was regularly taken to be a sign of a possible pregnancy. Samuel Pepys even began his famous diary, on 1 January 1660, with an entry describing how, since his wife Elizabeth hadn't had a period for seven weeks, the couple had begun to hope that she might be pregnant. However, on New Year's Eve Elizabeth started to bleed, dashing their hopes.

This idea even appears in an erotic novel *The London Jilt* (1683), a tale about a prostitute, Cornelia, who decides to trick a rich and besotted client into believing that she is pregnant. She tells him, 'undoubtedly I was with Child: For, added I to that, this was just the week I was to have had my courses [*period*]; and yet I had them not, which however never failed me one day in my life.' In the main, though, a pregnancy was never declared for certain until after quickening, the time when a woman first felt her child move in the womb, usually sometime between four and five months. This was a highly significant moment in a pregnancy because, for Protestants, it also marked the moment of 'ensoulment,' or when God had placed a living human soul into the foetus's body. Before this time the foetus was thought to be alive in the sense of an animal, awaiting the moment when God would implant its rational human side.

Multiple Births

Nicholas Culpeper wrote that, while Nature intended women to give birth to one child at a time, sometimes more babies were born during a single pregnancy. Following the fashion in medical books for narrating odd cases which had apparently happened abroad, both Culpeper and later Jane Sharp repeat the tale of Margaret, Countess of Henneberg (d. 1277) who, legend has it, gave birth to 364 living children at once.

Legends aside, two kinds of multiple pregnancy were thought to exist. The first type was thought to occur when the seed divided in the womb and made more than one baby, while the second theory, 'superfetation,' involved the womb of an already pregnant woman reopening during intercourse, letting in more seed and so creating another baby. This idea led to the belief that non-identical twins could have different fathers.

Sir Thomas Browne's 1646 book *Pseudodoxia Epidemica* claimed that there were numerous examples of this phenomenon in classical texts, including the writings of Pliny and Hippocrates, and explained how, by this process, the womb, 'after reception of its proper Tenant, may yet receive a strange and spurious inmate [...] as also in those superconceptions where one child was like the father, the other like the adulterer, the one favoured the servant, the other resembled the master.'

A multiple pregnancy was difficult to diagnose and was chiefly indicated by the size of the mother's abdomen. Sir Thomas Knyvett gossiped in a letter to his wife in November 1637, that the landlady of his lodgings, Margaret Elsynge, 'is extraordinarily big, as if she meant to have a couple.' Margaret had been married to Henry, a clerk at the House of Commons, for exactly a year at this point and went on to have at least five children, but there is no evidence whether or not this was a twin pregnancy.

Women with either a particularly large 'belly' or those who were carrying twins sometimes tied a scarf around their necks stretching under their stomachs to help support the weight. A French physician Ambroise Paré, whose work was available in English translation in the seventeenth century, wrote about an Italian woman named Dorothy, who allegedly had 20 children at just two births in the sixteenth century. He noted that she had had to tie a 'broad and large' scarf about her neck to support the weight of her heavily distended stomach, which rested on her knees.

Culpeper wrote that mixed sex twins were generally weaker than same sex ones. Medics were worried about women bearing twins having a more difficult labour, and Sharp advised midwives to bear in mind the possibility of superfetation; that the second twin might be significantly younger than the first and so should not be delivered unless it seemed ready. Sharp gave the example of a woman who gave birth to twins 15 weeks apart and advised that if there was no bleeding or signs of labour following the first twin, then the second one should be left alone.

Superstitions Surrounding Pregnancy

Thomas Raynalde wrote that if a pregnant woman wanted to discover whether she was carrying a 'man or a woman,' she should squeeze a drop of milk from her breast and let it fall on a shiny surface, like a knife. If the milk flowed freely then her child would be a girl, if it was more solid, a boy. Jane Sharp had a similar test which involved dropping some breast milk in a basin of water; if it floated then the woman was carrying a boy and if it sank, a girl. A less intrusive test was simply to note which foot a pregnant woman favoured when she got out of bed in the morning: the right foot indicated a boy and vice versa.

However, the test considered most reliable involved the belief that male babies were easier to carry, so a woman pregnant with a male foetus would walk more lightly on her feet, have a higher rounder bump, and generally look well. Sharp explained, 'the woman is more cheerful and in better health, her pains are not so often, nor so great, the right breast is harder and more plump, the nipple a more clear red, and the whole visage clear not swarthy.' Troublesome pregnancies were generally assumed to indicate that a girl was expected.

Medical authorities advised that pregnant women should aim to remain in a happy state of mind. Any ill thoughts and disturbing dreams or even external events were widely believed to have a detrimental effect on the foetus. Jane Sharp commented that many 'monstrous births' were caused by women looking at strange or inappropriate objects while pregnant. That women could bear monsters was not just the subject of sensational pamphlets, but routinely believed. Ralph Josselin noted in his diary that a monster had been born in Colchester in May 1646, which appeared like a child and a serpent and a toad all at once.

The power of the maternal imagination to affect the outcome of a pregnancy was widely perceived as beyond the medical texts. Sharp described this phenomenon:

Imagination can do much, as a woman that looked on a blackmore [black person] *brought forth a child like to a blackmore; and one that I knew, that seeing a boy with two thumbs on one hand, brought forth such another; but ordinarily the spirits and humours are disturbed by the passions of the mind, and so the forming faculty is hindered and overcome with too great plenty of humours that flow to the matrix* [womb].

The imagination was also used to explain physical deformities, such as cleft lips and palates. Thomas Lupton's 1589 miscellany, *A Thousand Notable Things*, claimed that for 'many women with child [*the*] sudden or unlooked for, meeting, or sudden seeing of a hare, or for the desire or longing to eat of the same: do bring forth children with a cloven over-lip, and forked-wise, called a hare lip.' Nicholas Culpeper's 1652 *Directory for Midwives* even went so far as to claim that if a pregnant woman, 'saw anything cut with a Cleaver, she brings forth a divided part or a Hare-lip.'

Sharp copied much of her medical theory from Culpeper's book (although she tempered his theories where they didn't fit with her years of experience as a midwife). In the case of hares causing cleft lips, she repeated Culpeper's anecdote and advice against this happening, and instructed pregnant women to 'slit her smock like her husband's shirt' to prevent this. This type of folk remedy comes from ancient medicine and superstition, and was thought to work by 'sympathy': you were saved from the adverse effect of such a sight when it was forced on to something or someone else.

In the same way frights or bad dreams were to be avoided by pregnant women. Isaac Archer described how, on 22 August 1676, his wife miscarried after receiving a shock: 'My wife miscarried again, through a sudden fright, upon an unhappy occasion, which I will not record, because 'twas beyond the intention of him that occasioned it.' Gentlewoman Alice Thornton also experienced a shock while pregnant, which caused a threatened miscarriage, and she thought, left a mark on the baby. Thornton almost caught herself on a penknife, then much bigger than modern ones, and she described how 'the fear and dread apprehension thereof did cause a mark of deep bloody colour upon the child's heart, most pure and distinct.' The mark was, she claimed, a birthmark shaped like a small cut, with drops of blood sprinkled around it.

All these theories returned to the theory that women should behave appropriately during pregnancy, since anything they did or thought could be transferred onto their unborn children. As Jane Sharp put it, if 'some women with child will desire to steal things from others,' in such a case the child would grow up to be a thief. Therefore, even in the womb, it was instilled in women that their child should be taught by example that moderation in all things was best and to fear God.

Antenatal Care

There was no direct early modern equivalent of the antenatal care a pregnant woman receives today. A woman would discuss her impending birth and 'book' the midwife, but if all was going well then a woman usually first sent for a midwife when she went into labour. If she fell ill during the pregnancy, she would consult a doctor or her midwife but most would not see any medical practitioner if all was progressing well.

Alice Thornton was regularly ill throughout her pregnancies, but once became caught between two doctors, who couldn't agree whether bloodletting was appropriate in pregnancy because of the concern that the baby needed blood for its nourishment. A Mr Mahum, who she described as her 'old doctor,' would not bleed her because of her advanced state of pregnancy, but after a further 11 days of fever and now losing her sight, she sent for a new physician, Dr Wittie, who agreed to let her blood. Alice recorded that she had had 'six or seven ounces taken,' after which she regained her sight.

Pregnant women were expected to look after all the external factors affecting their health, such as appropriate nutrition, sleeping properly, abstaining from intercourse, and living quietly. One practical step recommended by Nicholas Culpeper involved wearing a linen cloth soaked in almond oil (sometimes called a 'bellyband') around the abdomen to prevent 'wrinkles of the belly' or stretch marks.

The successful outcome of a pregnancy was largely ascribed to women's behaviour while she was expecting. However, women were not reproached when things went wrong and a pregnancy ended in a still birth as, in common with all life events, the outcome of a pregnancy was largely considered to be God's will and to be accepted unquestioningly.

Chapter Nine

Giving Birth

T he birth of a baby is a time that many women approach with mixed feelings: excitement and joy at the thought of the new addition to the family but, at the same time, trepidation for the birth itself. The process of giving birth is a hard and often painful one; it is called 'labour' for a reason.

Indeed, many women with experience of giving birth might identify with a seventeenth century mother of nine, Yorkshire gentlewoman Alice Thornton, who remembered the pain of labour as resembling being 'on the rack,' the medieval instrument of torture which stretched unfortunate prisoners limb from limb. Thornton was reminiscing about giving birth to her fifth child in the mid-seventeenth century, but the metaphor was a regular one, appearing, for example, in Jane Sharp's 1671 midwifery guidebook.

This chapter explores the ways that women prepared for and experienced labour and birth in the early modern era. Much of the information here is taken from Jane Sharp's book, because it was intended as a textbook for trainee midwives and to save inexperienced practitioners from mistaken beliefs or ill-informed midwifery care. The resulting book, subtitled *The Whole Art of Midwifry Discovered*, drew extensively on the works of contemporary medical writers and doctors, such as Daniel Sennert and Nicholas Culpeper, but these borrowings were not taken wholesale. Often she amended the doctors' words to accord more closely her thirty years' practice.

Jane Sharp's work was the first female-authored book on the topic to be produced in English and, unusually, it gives a female voice to a subject that women inevitably had the most experience of.

Calculating a 'Due Date' and Making Preparations

Any estimate of the date that a woman was due to give birth, or lie-in as it was then expressed, of course could not be as specific as a modern scan and other measures. Yet, Jane Sharp complained that women compounded their own uncertainty by not taking careful enough note of when their last period had occurred:

> *Young women especially of their first Child, are so ignorant commonly, that they cannot tell whether they have conceived or not, and not one in twenty keeps a just account, else they would be better provided against the time of their lying in, and not so suddenly surprised as many of them are.*

Generally, women knew roughly how many months pregnant they were though and had an approximate expectation of the month when they would deliver the baby. Before the birth a new mother would need to prepare the layette, known as making preparations against the time of delivery, and accumulate all the linen that the baby would need. All the baby's clothing and bedding had to be sewn by hand.

Such preparations were not merely a matter of practicality, but essential if anything untoward should happen to the baby during birth. If the woman went into labour unexpectedly and delivered a stillborn child, then she might be accused of having murdered it, but if she could show that she had gathered together an appropriate amount of 'childbed linen,' then this provided an accepted defence that she was prepared for the birth and ready for the baby's arrival.

The Onset of Labour

When a woman felt her 'throes' or labour pains start, the advice offered by authorities like Sharp seems very modern. Sharp counselled women in 'travail' to walk about their chambers or lie down, whichever option seemed most comfortable, but stressed that they should try to remain as active and warm as possible. All early modern women gave birth at home, as there was no concept of a hospital, let alone a maternity ward, that we would recognise.

The new mother would not have to face the event alone though, as births were a female social event and a woman would have a party made up of her friends, neighbours, and family surrounding her, supporting her in labour. These women were known as 'gossips,' a name which derived from the phrase 'god's helpers.' Men were mostly excluded from the process. When Jane Josselin went into labour around midnight on 24 November 1645, her minister husband Ralph called on one of his neighbours, Goodman Potter, to fetch the midwife, but waited until daylight to call 'the women,' Jane's gossips. He noted that 'almost all came' and Jane was delivered between 11 am and 12 pm that day.

The midwife would arrive carrying her bag, which contained oils, medicines and some tools, but also various cloths for different tasks. In 1682, A. Marsh joked that a midwife might offer 'warmed beds and other clouts, the number and names where of are without end.' When the midwife entered the house, the first thing she would usually do was to pray for the safe delivery of the woman and child. The threat of death was never far from the early modern birthing chamber, despite the fact that the vast majority of births were problem free.

After getting married in her mid-twenties, the average woman could expect to give birth around five times. The maternal mortality rate was around 1 per cent per pregnancy, lower than is often supposed. Maternal mortality rates were much higher in Victorian England, for example, at over 4 per cent and the reasons for this are many but are thought to include that the increasing medicalisation of birth in which physicians attended deliveries after seeing infected patients, without changing their clothes or washing, meant that newly delivered mothers were more susceptible to post-partum infections.

The main difference brought about by modern medical care is in births involving complications; in the early modern era, if something went wrong during the course of the labour, the chances of a woman and her child surviving were very much lower. Most women would have known, or at least heard of, someone who had died in a delivery. Some of the women whose memoirs and letters appear in this book died in this way. Maria Thynne died in 1611, while giving birth to the youngest of her three sons. Alice Thornton had nine births, yet only three of her children reached adulthood, and she always approached birth with fear, perhaps informed by the memory of her sister, Lady Katherine Danby, who died in 1645 giving birth to her sixteenth child.

Lady Katherine bore 10 live and six stillborn babies; her eldest son Thomas (b. 1631) went on to become the first mayor of Leeds. Alice described how

Katherine's final labour was traumatic from the outset, because her sister was missing her husband, who was away fighting the King's cause in the English Civil War and had been refused permission to return home. Lady Katherine laboured for 14 nights, according to Alice's account, but at last she delivered a healthy son – her fourteenth boy. As an added difficulty, she had not been able to use her regular midwife, who was shut up in Richmond, Yorkshire while the town was sealed following a plague outbreak. Instead, another midwife known as Dame Swore took on the role and delivered Francis, named after an earlier son who had died.

Lady Katherine died a month later of fever, having never recovered from the birth. Alice was particularly upset that Sir Thomas, her brother-in-law, had refused to let his wife receive the sacrament when he knew she was dying, perhaps because as a fervent Protestant from a family of Catholic recusants, he found such practices abhorrent. Lady Katherine was even denied a funeral service, because she was from a Royalist family. The headquarters of the Scottish forces on the side of Parliament were based in the area of Richmond where they lived, and they refused permission for a service to be held for her.

Other women too were often naturally apprehensive about an approaching labour. Ralph Josselin recorded that before several of his wife's labours, she was bothered with 'many sad fears.' Women often reflected upon the possibility of death in childbirth within some of the poetry they wrote. Anne Bradstreet (1612–1672), America's first published poet, who left England with the Puritan migration in 1630, wrote touchingly about this issue in her poem, 'Before the Birth of One of Her Children' (posthumously published in 1678). In this poem, Anne addresses her husband Simon, 'How soon, my Dear, death may my steps attend,/How soon't may be thy lot to lose thy friend.'

Anne accepted that her husband would remarry if anything happened to her, but pleaded with him to look after their children as his main priority:

> *And when thy loss shall be repaid with gains,*
> *Look to my little babes, my dear remains.*
> *And if thou love thy self, or loved'st me,*
> *These O protect from step-dame's injury.*

While potential medical interventions, such as Caesarean section, were known about in this period, they were strictly used for attempting to save the life of a child if the mother died in labour. If this became necessary, then it was considered essential to keep the woman's mouth and legs wide open, to allow the passage of air to the child whilst it was delivered. For this procedure it is almost certain that a doctor would have been sent for, as in most problematic labours. However, midwives were used dealing with all eventualities; Jane Sharp even gives a vivid description of how to extract a stillborn baby from the womb with the use of gruesome-sounding, but necessary, hooks.

Care in Labour and Delivery

The name midwife comes from a literal translation of the German phrase 'with woman' and, as this name suggests, the midwife would stay with a labouring woman throughout the birth and delivery. Jane Sharp advised midwives to keep the labouring woman's spirits up with comforting words, which was also one of the tasks carried out by the 'gossips' or attendants.

Some pain was expected in labour and broadly accepted as God's will, a consequence of Eve's transgression in the Garden of Eden. As John Marten rather sanctimoniously put it in his 1711 book on venereal disease, 'if the first Woman Eve, had not sinned, she had never been exposed to the Pangs of Child-birth, nor to the Shame, nor Confusion of seeing herself defiled once a Month with her own impure Blood.'

However, most medical guides suggested remedies providing pain-relief for women enduring extremely hard labours. Certain types of women were thought more likely to have uncomfortable labours, including the very young, the 'gross and fat' and conversely, those who were 'spare and lean,' according to Thomas Raynalde in 1545. Raynalde's tips for easing labour pains are mainly concerned with trying to speed up the delivery. He recommended various things, from oiling the private parts, to 'suffumigations,' which consisted of medicines heated on hot coals to produce a specific smoke or 'fume,' intended to open up the labouring mother's body. A pessary dipped in the herb rue was also offered as a method to speed up the labour. Raynalde gave the recipes for various pills considered to help the woman give birth 'without pain.' These tablets are also mainly concerned with speeding up the birth, although one recipe does contain opiates and is meant to be drunk with some 'good wine,' so it might well have provided some relief.

To help a labour along, midwives sometimes applied an eagle stone to the woman's private parts. An eagle stone was a hollow, round stone with a smaller stone inside, signifying the pregnant woman and her unborn child. But, as Sharp warned, the stone was thought to be so powerful that it should be removed as soon as the afterbirth was delivered, or it might cause the woman harm. Other practices intended to help labour along included herbal drinks made up of betony, sage, or other suitable herbs. To assist the birth or to draw down the afterbirth, the midwife might have administered pepper to cause a sneezing fit, or advised a woman to hold her breath, to encourage the baby to come out to seek air. If the woman had been in labour a long time and needed sustenance, then she might be fed chicken broth, or a poached egg, with a little wine or other strong water.

Later on in a labour, the gossips often helped to hold the woman up as she was about to deliver; they might also be encouraged to stroke the pregnant woman's belly in a downward motion, to encourage the baby to move into the birth canal. Of course, at the opposite extreme, sometimes the baby came too fast for the midwife to get there in time.

Jane Josselin's fourth child, Ralph, was born 'an hour and a half before day' on the morning of 11 February 1648, but came so fast that she was only attended by her five gossips. This was repeated the following May, when she came to give birth to her next child, also called Ralph, after the previous child who had died after just 10 days. As her husband commented, 'some few women were with her but the midwife not, but when God commands deliverance there is nothing hinders it.'

The Delivery

There was no single conventional position for women to give birth in, but Jane Sharp advised that very fat women should be encouraged to kneel face down to give birth. Some women lay on the bed, propped up by their gossips, others used a birthing stool or sat on the side of the bed. A birthing stool was a horse shoe shaped chair, on which a woman could sit while the birth progressed. Although Thomas Raynalde wrote that stools like this were more common on the Continent, English midwives sometimes owned one and carried it to the delivery chamber.

The delivery room was carefully prepared and kept draught-free and warm, but the idea that women were shut up in airless, overheated, dark rooms is a misconception. The midwife would cover her hand with an oil of lilies or almonds, or a little grease such as butter, and perform internal examinations to ascertain the position of the child in the womb. The midwife might keep her hand inside the woman from then on, to be in a position to help when the baby started to come.

The waters surrounding the baby were thought to make delivery easier if they broke on the point of delivery, since they made the birth canal more slippery. If this had already happened, then it was suggested that the woman's vagina should be smeared with egg, or more oil of lilies to help the birth on. Sharp warned her sister midwives not to force the baby out for fear of harming the mother or child, and of causing the woman terrible pain.

After the baby was born and the afterbirth, or 'womb-cake' as it was often called, was delivered, the midwife had several further tasks to perform. If the labour had been particularly hard, then she might wrap the woman's back in a newly-flayed sheepskin, presumably to keep her warm and comfortable. It was also considered good practice after deliveries to lay a hare skin covered in the animal's blood, on the mother's belly for two hours in winter and an hour in summer. This gruesome measure was thought to help close up the womb. Afterwards the stomach was wiped down with the oil of St John's Wort. A linen pad was sometimes placed inside the woman to raise the womb and encourage it to return to its normal situation. The woman was then covered in sheets and encouraged to lie still for 10 to 12 hours to let her blood settle.

However, she was not allowed to go to sleep for the first four hours, and instead was nourished with a little broth and some watered-down wine. Nicholas Culpeper and other physicians also advised that if a woman had a lot of stretch marks, then an ointment made from sperm whale wax, oil of almonds and sheep suet, rubbed into the flesh would help to gradually refine the creases and reduce the loose skin. Most midwifery textbooks explained that women should bleed a certain amount after the birth, to remove the excess blood built up during the pregnancy, or they would not recover their health.

Sharp contended that it was unusual for a woman to bleed too much, but most guides to women's health sensationalised the risk of bleeding excessively. Sharp said that one of the reasons a woman might bleed too much was because some ignorant midwives rushed to give constipated new mothers medicines to open their bowels. Due to the way the humoral body was thought to work, this treatment was believed to encourage a general purge of the body, with blood surging out of the body along with the faeces.

The Father's Role During a Birth

Although the birthing room was an all-female environment, unless things went wrong and a doctor had to be called in, fathers-to-be were still anxious about the process, and many joyful letters survive from fathers announcing their new arrivals. John Hervey, earl of Bristol wrote to his cousin after the birth of his last child, Henrietta, in September 1716, 'my wife was safely brought to bed between 4 and 5 this morning of a girl, and though the largest of all the twenty children God has blessed me with.'

God had answered Hervey's prayers that his wife might have a swift and 'favourable' birth. Not all fathers were as supportive as they might have been though, and clergyman Isaac Archer recorded in his diary in November 1670 how his wife had the 'show' or small loss of blood that often marks the onset of labour, but because it was Sunday he was unwilling to be distracted, and so requested that she not disturb him; poor Anne Archer kept quiet until 8 pm. Anne experienced a particularly difficult labour because the baby was born in the posterior position (face-up), and it was also much 'fatter and stronger' than their last daughter.

However, a few years later, at another birth, Archer recorded a stillborn daughter in October 1677, writing that, 'about 4 of the clock in the afternoon my wife was delivered, 2 months before her reckoning, and of a girl, which came wrong, and stuck so long with the head in the birth, that it was dead when fully borne, though alive in the time of travail [*labour*].' Archer's overriding concern at this birth was for his wife's health, and he gave thanks to God that she was 'hearty' and likely to make a full recovery.

Care for the Newborn

After delivering the baby and settling the mother, a midwife still had a number of jobs to do. The umbilical cord (or naval string) needed to be cut at four fingers' distance from the body. A myth stated that the longer the cord left on a male infant, the longer his manhood would be in later life – and since Jane Sharp stated unequivocally that men with long penises were fools, and leaving too long a cord was not encouraged in her book. Similarly, women who had difficulty giving birth might blame the midwife who delivered them for cutting their cords too short and subsequently making their 'secret parts' too small.

The child's naval was then anointed with ash and covered in lint, to help it to dry and keep the cold out. Newborn babies were then swaddled, or bound from head to toe in rags which needed changing regularly to keep the baby warm and dry. Swaddling bands were used for around four months, to encourage the child's limbs to grow strong and straight. This practice was common from antiquity until the later eighteenth century when it went out of fashion. Babies' swaddling bands were changed frequently, so that babies did not get nappy rash or, as it was then known, 'galling of children.'

John Pechey's childhood diseases book (1697), explained that galling was uncommon in children who were frequently changed, but prevalent in neglected babies, and in some cases the skin of the hips and genitals could be 'fretted off' due to the acrimony of the urine. Pechey gave a recipe for a soothing bath made from bran and marshmallows, followed by a powder made from rose and frankincense, which was intended to ease galling.

Postnatal Care

Women did not suckle their babies for the first few days of their lives, as early modern women were distrustful of 'colostrum' or first milk. This is understandable, as it looks watery and odd-coloured, not at all like milk. This was a shame for the mother and the baby, as we are now aware of the vital antibodies and other nutrients it contains. Ideally, the new mother's bedroom would be kept quite dark for three days, because her eyes were thought to be quite weak after the birth. Each day, for the first week, the midwife would bathe the woman's genitalia with herbal water to cleanse and heal her.

After a week, the mother's bed sheets or the straw that made up her bed could safely be changed, but the woman was still advised to keep to her bed for a few more days. On the whole, most women adhered to the practice of the 'woman's month' to a greater or lesser extent. Elite women might lie-in for up to six weeks, as alluded to by the prostitute Cornelia in the 1680s erotic novel *The London Jilt* when she comments after her delivery that, having been left a pension by her deceased lover she, 'followed the example of persons of condition and kept state [*or lay-in*] for six weeks.'

Lady Ann Fanshawe had several pregnancies during the Civil War period and always observed a full lying-in period, even though this meant lengthy separations from her husband as he travelled in the King's service. During the women's month the restrictions of the lying-in period became less severe and women were often up and pottering in the house after a couple of weeks. Alice Thornton noted how she would sit up in a chair, 'giving my child suck,' after two weeks. Women whose work contributed to the family's income, of course, often couldn't afford to take the whole month off, and some were back weaving or taking in laundry after three weeks or less.

Churching: Recovery and Thanksgiving After a Birth

Officially, medical books and the Church both advised a period of 30 days' lying-in, if a woman gave birth to a boy or 60 for a girl, because a female child was thought to take longer to develop in the womb and so took longer for the woman to recover from carrying, but in practice few seem to have stuck to this rule. During the woman's month couples were forbidden from having sexual relations, and most appear to have observed this custom. The end of the woman's month was marked by a religious service known as 'churching.' The new mother would be taken to church by her midwife, husband, and gossips and a thanksgiving service for her safe delivery was performed.

At the service the vicar would recite special prayers, which were set out in the 1552 *Book of Common Prayer*. The service ended by the vicar intoning the following words:

O Almighty God, which hast delivered this woman thy servant from the great pain and peril of childbirth: Grant, we beseech thee (most merciful father,) that she through thy help, may both faithfully live and walk in her vocation, according to thy will in this life present; and also may be partaker of everlasting glory in the life to come: through Jesus Christ our Lord. Amen.

After the service the group would return to the new mother's house, or the local tavern, for a party, often a rowdy affair. The main significance of the day was to mark the woman's safe delivery and return into society after her ordeal. Yet, the day also marked the potential resumption of a couple's sex life – although, if the woman was still breastfeeding, then they were supposed to abstain from sex until the child was weaned.

The recommencement of marital sex after a birth was written about in erotic verse by poets such as Robert Herrick (1591–1674). One of Herrick's poems, 'Julia's Churching or Purification' (1648), describes how Julia put on the special clothes needed for the ceremony, included her 'Holy Fillitings'or veil. This poem made no mention of the after-party, as it is anticipating the marital reunion instead, 'Where ceremonious hymen shall for thee / Provide a second epithalamie.' In a similar vein, an early translation of Nicolas de Venette's book *The Mysteries of Conjugal Love Revealed* (1707), suggested that women looked forward to the resumption of their sex-life, writing that 'After travel [*labour*] and childbearing, the woman forgets the Pains that she suffered, her flood being no sooner stopped, but she attacks her husband afresh, and gives him an amorous battle.'

How far all women might have endorsed de Venette's comments is debatable, especially after a difficult birth, but for the majority of women the outcome of childbirth was a healthy baby, a couple of years of nursing and then starting the process all over again.

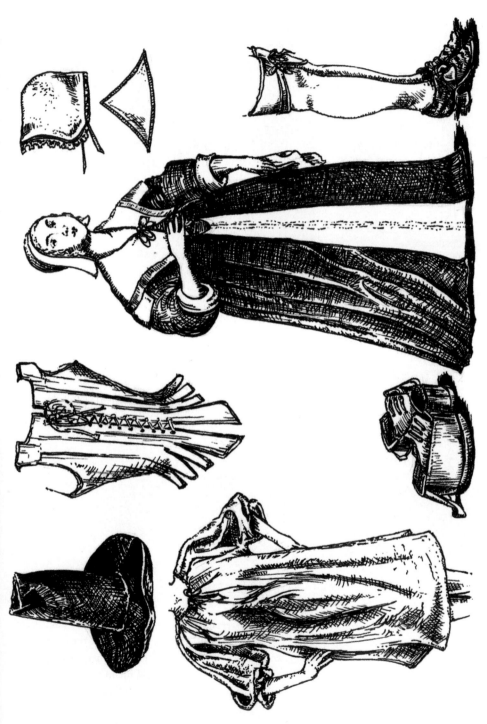

Illustration of seventeenth-century women's dress, featuring a *capotain* tall hat, a pair of stays, a coif, a partlet, gartered stockings and shoes, pattens, and the ubiquitous shift. (*Image © Rachel Adcock, 2014*)

Royal Women in the time covered by this book

Queen Elizabeth I of England, daughter of Henry VIII and Anne Boleyn. *(Wellcome Library, London)*

Queen Anne of Denmark, wife of James I of England. *(Wellcome Library, London)*

Queen Anne, second daughter of James II. *(Wellcome Library, London)*

Charles I, son of James I and Anne, with his wife Henrietta Maria. The marriage was childless, meaning James II was his brother's heir. *(Wellcome Library, London)*

Queen Mary II, elder daughter of James II, who took the crown in a joint reign with her husband and cousin, William of Orange, from her father following the Glorious Revolution of 1688. *(Wellcome Library, London)*

Marriage

Abraham Bosse, 'The workings and signing of a marriage contract' (1633). *(Wellcome Library, London)*

From the cover of *The Gentlewoman's Companion; or a Guide to the Female Sex* (1682), a guide to running a household, showing a likeness of the author Hannah Woolley. *(Wellcome Library, London)*

Ann Biddlestone, being punished in a scold's bridle. From Ralph Gardiner, *England's Grievance Discovered* (1655). *(Wellcome Library, London)*

Eleanor Rummings, a well known landlady of an ale-house. *(Wellcome Library, London)*

Cooking and Food preparation

Posset Pot from London dated 1661. *(Wellcome Library, London)*

Pages from Mrs Katherine Palmer, 'A Collection of ye best Receipts,' 1700–1739, pp 205–206. *(Wellcome Library, London)*

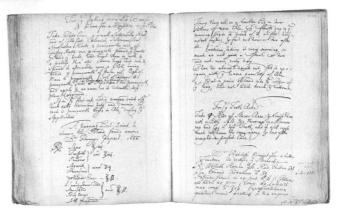

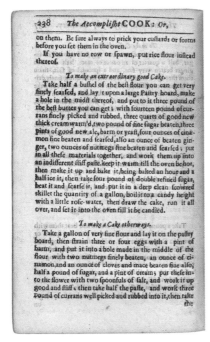

Recipe 'To make an extraordinary good cake.' From Robert May, *The Accomplisht Cook; or The Art and Mystery of Cookery* (1678), p. 238. *(Wellcome Library, London)*

'A woman hard at work distilling.' From J. S. *The Accomplished Ladies Rich Closet of Rarities; or, the Ingenious Gentlewoman and Servant-maid's Delightful Companion* (1691). *(Wellcome Library, London)*

Domestic scenes

One of the fireplaces at Selly Manor, Bourneville, Birmingham, dating from 1629, with a bread oven next to it. My thanks to Selly Manor for permission to take photographs in the building. *(Pete Read)*

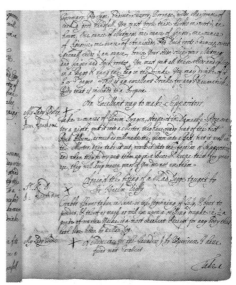

A recipe for making 'excellent suppositories' from Lady Ann Fanshawe's 'Recipe Book, containing Medical, Culinary and other Recipes, compiled from 1651.' *(Wellcome Library, London)*

An example of a tester bed on display in Selly Manor, showing the ropes which support the mattress. *(Pete Read)*

'Two witches smoking their pipes by the fire with a toad at their feet.' From *The History of Witches and Wizards* (1720), p. 3. *(Wellcome Library, London)*

Adriaen van Ostade, 'A Woman Breast-feeding her Child Amongst her Family' (1641). *(Wellcome Library, London)*

Pregnancy

Etching of three pregnant women, taken from a German medical text (1546). *(Wellcome Library, London)*

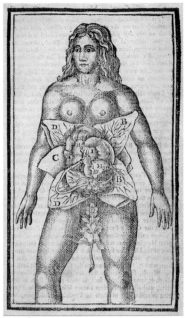

'A dissection of the womb' from Jane Sharp's *The Complete Midwives Companion* (1724). *(Wellcome Library, London)*

An Italian woman named Dorothy who reputedly had twenty children at to births. Drawn here pregnant with 'nine or eleven babies' using a bellyband to support the pregnancy. From Ambroise Paré, *The Works of that Famous Surgeon Amboise Parey* (1678). *(Wellcome Library, London)*

Figures of babies in the womb. From Eucharius Rösslin, *The Birth of Mankind* (1604), p. 110. *(Wellcome Library, London)*

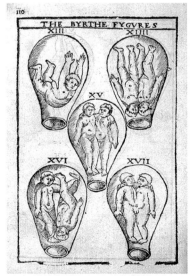

Giving birth

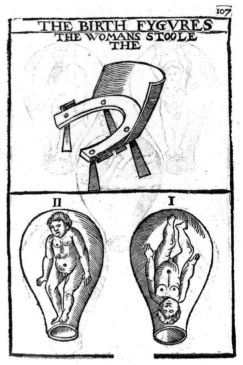

'A woman seated on a obstetrical chair giving birth aided by a midwife who works beneath her skirts.' From Eucharius Rösslin, *Rosengarten* (1513). *(Wellcome Library, London)*

Birthing stool and babies in the womb, from another edition of Eucharius Rösslin, *The Birth of Mankind* (1565). *(Wellcome Library, London)*

'Mr Giffard's extractor forceps as improved by Mr Freke.' From William Giffard's *Cases in Midwifry* (1734). *(Wellcome Library, London)*

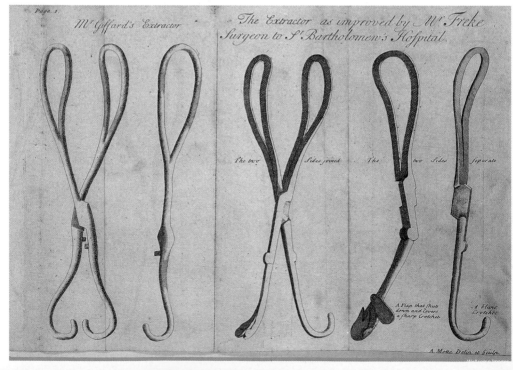

'A woman giving birth aided by a surgeon who fumbles beneath a sheet to save the lady from embarrassment' (1711). *(Wellcome Library, London)*

'A seated woman giving birth aided by a midwife and two other attendants, in the background two men are looking at the stars and plotting a horoscope' (1583). *(Wellcome Library, London)*

After the birth

Scene after the birth of a child. From Jakob Rüf, *De Conceptu et Generatione Hominis* (1580). *(Wellcome Library, London)*

The frontispiece to Jane Sharp's *The Complete Midwives Companion* (1724). The three scenes show a newly delivered woman, the baptism procession led by the midwife, and the celebration afterwards. *(Wellcome Library, London)*

Care of the Infant

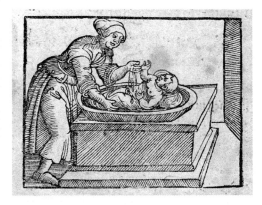

Bathing a baby (1546). *(Wellcome Library, London)*

Child with feeding bottle (1546). *(Wellcome Library, London)*

Child in a baby walker/playpen (1577). *(Wellcome Library, London)*

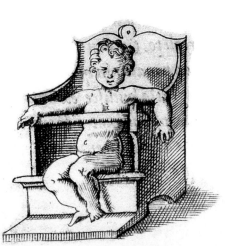

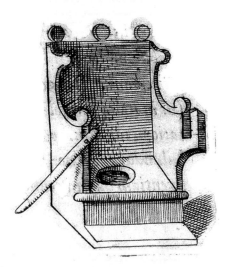

Child potty training (1577). *(Wellcome Library, London)*

Breasts and Breastfeeding

Francesco Cozza, 'Pero breastfeeding her father Cimon to assuage his hunger,' 17th Century. *(Wellcome Library, London)*

'Elizabeth Hopkins of Oxford, showing a breast with cancer which was removed by Sir William Read. Engraving by M. Burghers, ca. 1700.' *(Wellcome Library, London)*

Ann Clarke, aged 53, suffering from breast cancer. *(Wellcome Library, London)*

Medical Understandings

'Caricature of female barber-surgeons bloodletting from a patient's foot' (1695). *(Wellcome Library, London)*

'A cyster [an enema] in use. Oil painting by a French painter, ca. 1700.' *(Wellcome Library, London)*

A woman being let blood from her ankle (1623), a common treatment for menstrual problems. *(Wellcome Library, London)*

'The doctor's dispensary and the apothecary's shop in the 17th century.' From Nicolas Culpeper's translation of *The Expert Doctors Dispensatory* (1657). *(Wellcome Library, London)*

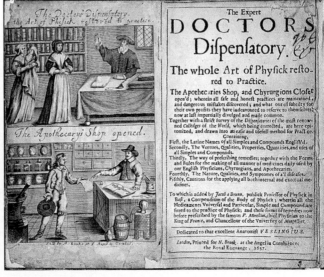

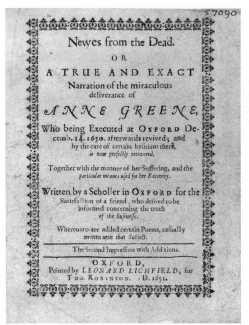

'Title page of 'News from the Dead,' a book of poetry about Anne Greene who was executed at Oxford and afterwards revived' by Richard Watkins (1651). *(Wellcome Library, London)*

'Mary Tofts [or Toft], a woman who pretended that she had given birth to rabbits. Coloured stipple engraving by Maddocks (1819).' *(Wellcome Library, London)*

John and Mary Champian, depicted after Mary murdered their son. *(The Lewis Walpole Library, Yale University)*

'Sarah Malcolm sitting in prison with her hands resting on a table. Engraving by T. Cook after W. Hogarth' (1802). *(Wellcome Library, London)*

Grand homes

The ruins of Brampton Bryan Castle, Herefordshire which was the home of the Harley family. The castle was besieged and attacked in 1643 during the first English civil war. *(Pete Read)*

Brampton Bryan Castle: the upper storey is thought to have been Brilliana, Lady Harley's chamber. *(Pete Read)*

Aston Hall, Birmingham, built by Sir Thomas Holte between 1618 and 1635. Although she didn't live here, the Dionys Fitzherbert lodged with the family for a time. *(Pete Read)*

Homes of the up and coming Middling Sort

Blakesley Hall, Yardley, Birmingham dates from 1590, and was built by Richard Smalbroke of one of the rising merchant class families. *(Pete Read)*

Selly Manor, Bourneville, Birmingham, showing the overhanging eaves typical of houses from this time. The eaves allowed upstairs rooms to be larger than downstairs. People sheltering under the eaves could often hear what was being said in the room above, from where the phrase 'eaves-dropping' derives. *(Pete Read)*

Little Moreton Hall, Congleton, which was enlarged in 1610 in line with the Moreton's increasing wealth. The rather precariously built glass windowed long gallery is designed for exercising in bad weather but also shows the rising status of the family. *(Pete Read)*

A priest hole, to hide illegal Catholic priests, can be seen in the attic rooms of Selly Manor. *(Pete Read)*

Chapter Ten

Breastfeeding and Hiring a Wet Nurse

Today, during antenatal care an expectant mother is actively encouraged to breastfeed her child. Not only do midwives and other health professionals promote this, but she will also be given a plethora of pamphlets and supporting material explaining the benefits of nursing her baby when the time comes. The sort of texts the modern pregnant woman reads would not be familiar to the seventeenth century expectant mother, but pamphlets urging them to breastfeed might well have been.

The doctor and medical writer Helkiah Crooke suggested, in 1615, that breastfeeding was part of what we now see as the bonding process. While breastfeeding, he speculated, 'the Mother doth not only nourish her Infants, but embraces them and kisses them; and so love being never forgotten, at length grows reciprocal and mutual.'

Both medical books and popular pamphlets discussing the advantages of breastfeeding appeared during the seventeenth century. The alternative for mothers who did not wish to breastfeed then was, of course, not formula milk, but feeding them at another woman's breast. Wet nurses were widely used throughout the period, especially amongst higher-ranking women who seldom nursed their own babies. Elizabeth Clinton, Countess of Lincoln published a short book in 1622 called *The Countess of Lincoln's Nursery*, urging mothers to breastfeed their own children rather than putting them out to be nursed by other women. Clinton claimed to regret bitterly not having fed any of her 18 children herself.

The Countess was not the first author to make this point, in fact she was following a tradition which can be traced to the humanist Catholic priest Desiderius Erasmus, whose Latin text *Puerpera, or the New Mother* (1526) referred to women who did not breastfeed as 'half-mothers.' Elizabeth Clinton had many reasons for not nursing her own children, but her decision was largely due to her husband's wish that she should not breastfeed. She wrote that:

partly I was overruled by another's authority, and *partly deceived by some* [one]*'s ill counsel,* & *partly I had not so well considered of my duty in this motherly office.*

A husband's command was the main reason that many women gave for employing another woman to breastfeed their children. The link between breastfeeding and the lack of menstrual periods was well understood at this time, and so a husband keen on having a large family would want his wife to become fertile again at the earliest opportunity, even if this meant that she should not breastfeed their latest child. Conversely, it was thought that if a woman should happen to become pregnant while she was still breastfeeding this would be very damaging for the nursling, because the foetus would absorb all the nutrients, and so the older child might become weak and sickly. Both outcomes saw many men of the higher ranks insist that their children be fed by women other than their wives.

Lady Elizabeth Hervey, the second wife of the earl of Bristol could not have breastfed her 17 children, since they were all born during an 18-year period. Indeed two of her sons, Thomas and William, were born almost exactly 11 months apart (on 20 January and 25 December 1699). Elizabeth kept her babies and their nurses close by her though, writing to her husband on April 1715, that their second youngest child Lady Louisa had been very well-behaved on a recent coach journey, as she didn't cry but merely 'whimpered only when she wanted the bubby [*breast*].'

Other reasons women gave for not wanting to breastfeed might seem surprisingly modern. It was commonly thought that the breastfeeding might spoil a woman's figure and make her chest sag. There has never been any medical evidence to support this conjecture, but the same argument is still given by some today. Linked to this fear was the idea that breastfeeding could age a woman prematurely. Another concern that new mothers expressed was the potential damage to their clothing from nursing, and milk staining expensive garments. The Countess of Lincoln thought this argument too ridiculous or 'unworthy' to warrant an answer, but she went on to say that ladies should 'behold most nursing mothers, and they be as clean and sweet in their clothes, and carry their age, and hold their beauty, as well as those that suckle not: and most likely are they so to do.'

Some women simply considered breastfeeding beneath them, and saw it as an act of manual labour, unfitting for a woman of rank to perform. Fathers, as well as husbands, would rue hearing the news that their daughters had decided to nurse their own child, fearing that it would reflect badly on their status, in an era when social status was meant to be demonstrated in your behaviour. Having insufficient milk or being too weak to nurse were other justifications given by upper-ranking women.

Author and midwife Jane Sharp lent a cynical ear to these excuses, as she disapproved of wet nursing, calling it a 'remedy that needs a remedy.' Sharp gave an example, which is probably about a wet nurse employed by either Charles II or James II, to support her assertion that a lack of milk was not a proper reason for failing to breastfeed your baby. Sharp recounted that the Royal physicians wanted to sack one nurse when she was deemed to have insufficient milk to nourish her young charge. According to Sharp's anecdote, the nurse was defended by King Charles I, who said, 'is not a pint of cream as good as a quart of milk?'

The main reason that Elizabeth Clinton and others were especially keen to encourage women to breastfeed their own children was because they considered it to be God's will. As Clinton put it, 'God provides milk in our breasts against the time of our children's birth, and this he hath done ever since it was said to us also, increase and multiply.' However, even the most zealous advocates of breast feeding acknowledged that not every woman received God's favour and with it the 'blessings of the breast as well as that of the womb.'

In December 1670, Anne Archer had to place her newborn daughter, also Anne, with a nurse briefly, because, despite the fact that the baby would 'suck greedily of others,' she could not latch on to her mother, 'by reason of her short nipples, and the [baby's] tongue not so long as in some.' According to her husband, the couple 'despaired of what I had so desired of God, the blessings of the breast as well as that of the womb; and my wife was resolving to try no more.' However, through God's intervention, Archer claimed,

'When she thought not of it, the child took the breast, and so continued; which we look on as a remarkable providence of our God!'

It is important to remember that there was not the same attitude to sharing breast milk in the past as there is now. Indeed, if the elderly or frail were struggling to receive nourishment, then it was quite normal for a nursing mother to feed them at her breast to aid their recovery. Minister Ralph Josselin recorded in his diary how, after the birth of his son Ralph in February 1648, the child only lived 10 days, and his wife was in some discomfort at the 'turning of her milk.' Yet, fortuitously it had not quite dried up when they heard that 'Old Mrs Harkenden was likely to die,' and so Jane Josselin was able to give the elderly woman some of her milk. It wasn't enough to save her though, and she died six days later. Josselin doesn't record what his wife, then grieving for a son who had died only three days previously, felt at having to nurse a dying woman, but he described it as a blessing that 'the good Lord fit her for that charge.'

Similarly, in his plea for release from gaol, in June 1627 political prisoner Sir Francis Barrington sent the court a physician's report claiming that he was so weak of consumption – which he blamed on the conditions of his imprisonment – that, despite having 'sucked a woman's breast these five weeks,' his doctor didn't expect him to live long.

Employing a wet-nurse was not just the preserve of the rich, and it was the norm for a baby to be fed by someone other than its mother for the first few days of its life, even if the mother intended to nurse it herself in the future. It was universally believed that it would be harmful for a child to drink the first milk a woman produces after she had given birth. This early milk was known to early moderns as 'beestings' and while the mother was waiting for her ordinary milk to come through, her child was fed by another nursing woman, often a friend or neighbour with an older child whose milk was considered safe for the newborn.

Lady Anne Clifford noted, with some pride, in 1654 that her daughter Margaret, the Countess of Thanet had been present at the birth of Lady Anne's first great-grandchild. This aristocratic family now promoted maternal nursing and since Lady Margaret had herself only had a daughter nine weeks previously, she was able to nurse her granddaughter until the mother's milk came in. Lady Anne then noted that her granddaughter, Lady

Margaret Coventry, continued to maternally nurse, as her own mother had done.

The new mother would have her initial breast milk [*colostrum*] extracted by the midwife with cupping glasses, or according to some midwifery guides, she might even use a newly whelped puppy to suckle, to ensure she kept producing milk until it was deemed appropriate for her to take over the nursing of her newborn. Anne Archer, who struggled to get her baby to latch on because of her inverted nipples, attempted to use a puppy. However, when her husband brought her a puppy, she 'could not make it lay hold,' which gave the couple the impression that if even the puppy failed to latch on then breastfeeding was not going to be possible. However, the situation righted itself, and Anne was able to nurse her baby soon after.

Thomas Raynalde recommended getting another person to suck nipples in such cases, and it is significant that Jane Sharp left out any mention of puppies as aids for nursing mothers in her guide, despite the fact that the advice appeared in some of her sources. Evidently this was not something she held with, or perhaps it did not strike her as much of a solution.

Choosing a Wet Nurse

For women who intended to put their child out to nurse for the long-term, many health manuals contain lists of the ideal characteristics a potential wet nurse should possess, to help the parents recruit the best candidate. Sharp's *Midwives Book* lists the criteria required, acknowledging that, despite her personal disapproval of it, the practice of employing wet nurses was widespread among the rich. It was considered essential that a wet nurse should have the correct humoral disposition for the job, as evidenced by a clear, ruddy complexion (as she was believed to pass this on to the child), possess a good constitution, and be aged between 18 and 40. If possible, the nurse should also resemble the birth mother as much possible.

For Sharp, the main risk in putting out a child to nurse was that the child would take on the natural disposition of the nurse through drinking her milk. So it was important, Sharp advised, to steer clear of any nurse who was 'crooked, or squint-eyed, nor with a misshapen nose, or body, or with black ill-favoured teeth, or stinking breath, or with any notable depravation [*or appearance of disease*].' There were a lot of characteristics to take into consideration in employing a nurse, for even minor defects like short-sightedness were believed to be transferable with breast milk.

Any prospective nurse would be subjected to an intimidating range of personal inspections designed to ensure that she had 'handsome breasts and nipples,' was not too thin nor too fat, nor excessively tall or short, and her veins were visible through her skin. Even her hair colour was taken into account, with the most suitable shade reckoned to be somewhere on the spectrum between red and black, although not an extreme shade, and ideally a light brown with natural highlights. Above all, parents would make sure that their prospective nurse had delivered a child of the same sex as their own. This presumably meant that a nurse could not be employed in advance of a birth, as with the dry nurse and the cradle rockers employed in the nursery of every woman of rank.

The idea that the characteristics of a nurse passed to the child along with her milk crops up in an anecdote told by author Daniel Defoe. In *The Complete English Gentleman*, which remained unpublished until the late nineteenth century, Defoe claimed that Queen Anne of Denmark (1574–1619), the wife of James I, had nursed her babies against aristocratic norms. Defoe attributes the following words to her, 'will I let my child, the child of a king, suck the milk of a subject and mingle the royal blood with the blood of a servant. No! No! The son of a king should suck none but the milk of a queen.'

After physical characteristics, employers tried to check the personality traits of a prospective nurse. She should be cheerful and friendly, willing to sing and dance, never depressive or fretful. Ideally, she should be well educated, according to her rank, but it was more important that she should delight in the company of children. The nurse was also required to possess a modest demeanour and, if married, she should not 'accompany with' her husband for the duration of her employment, up to two years, because if she was to become pregnant, then the foetus would take nutrients away from the nursling.

An appropriate personality was the main concern for Elizabeth Joscelin (1595–1622) when employing a wet nurse. Elizabeth wrote a book, *The Mother's Legacy to her Unborn Child* (1624), published two years after her death, which ran to at least three editions. The book was designed to guide the child should its mother die in childbirth, which was exactly what transpired in her own case, as Elizabeth died just nine days after giving birth to a daughter, Theodora. Elizabeth went against the prescriptions of the medical books in her 'legacy' to her unborn child, and asked her husband to ensure that if she died in childbirth, he would find a 'religious nurse no matter what her complexion.' Her priority was for the prospective nurse's pious personality to transfer to the nursling, ahead of any concerns about her humoral make up.

Although Jane Sharp did not endorse the practice of wet nursing she didn't rule it out altogether, especially if the new mother had sore or infected breasts and could not feed her newborn. She also saw that, for a poor woman who had a plentiful supply of milk, selling her excess milk in the form of wet nursing could form a useful income stream: 'if they be poor, for it will help them with food, and not hurt her own child.' In this scenario the poor woman could make enough money by wet nursing to supplement the family's food bill.

John Dee (1527–1609), the famous Elizabethan mathematician and mystic, recorded paying the wet nurses of his eight children differing amounts between 4-12 shillings a month, plus soap and candles, to nurse his children in their own homes. Clergyman William Gouge (1575–1653) paid 2 shillings and 6 pence per week in 1622. In 1639, Robert Woodforde (1606–1654) paid 40 shillings, plus 2s 6d, to his wet nurse, which was, presumably, for the entire six months' work that she had done, but as the nurse was also taking her nursling away with her, she could expect future payments too. In 1647 Sir Ralph Verney (1616–1696) paid a wet nurse 4 shillings a week and two loads of wood.

The wealthier the family a wet nurse served the higher the potential rewards were, with the nurses of royalty being the highest remunerated. In aristocratic families, the nurse moved into their household and so had bed and board provided on top of her salary. There were many reasons for this, including security of the child and concerns that if the child died, it might be substituted by the nurse's own baby so she did not lose her income.

A treatise on the state of the nation by Edward Chamberlayne, published in 1669, lists the expenses incurred by the Duke of Cambridge's nursery. Edgar, Duke of Cambridge, who died in infancy, was the second of James

II's sons to bear this title. Chamberlayne quoted accounts showing that the child's wet nurse was paid £80 in one year, the same figure paid to a dry nurse. This was unusual, as the dry nurse was usually paid substantially less than the wet nurse. As befitted his royal status as an heir to his uncle's throne, Cambridge's nursery bill was large for, in addition to the wet and dry nurses, three rockers were also employed, at £70 each. To put this into some context the 'necessary woman,' who emptied the chamber pots, received £50, and the cook £38 and 5 shillings.

The normal arrangement was for the child to be sent out to the wet nurse's home, which was often located in the countryside as this was felt to provide a healthier environment than the city. Parents would record in their diaries trips they took to visit the child at nurse. Robert Woodforde noted that in July 1639, just under two months since his daughter Sarah was taken home by her nurse, that he went to visit her and was pleased to find her very well. This seems to have been common among other early modern fathers too. John Dee, for example, went to see his children out at nurse every month or two.

In the grandest households where the wet nurse became a live-in household servant, while her own child might be put out to nurse with another woman while she gave all her milk to suckle the child of a wealthier woman. The Countess of Lincoln objected to this practice and felt that it disparages the character of women who were willing to work as wet nurses. How could one trust the character of a woman who would '*estrange* herself from her *own child*, to give suck to the *nurse-child*,' she asked. Taking a more sympathetic tack, the Countess also suggested that would be natural for a woman who has given up her child to nurse someone else's to become fretful, which might harm the nursling. She argued that a richer woman should not tempt a poorer woman with a high fee to 'banish her own infant.'

Neglectful Wet Nurses

There are many anecdotal stories about the problems of leaving a child in the charge of a woman from outside the family, who would not have the same emotional commitment to the baby in her care, as a mother. In her anti-wet nurse propaganda, Elizabeth Clinton claimed to have only employed two good wet nurses out of all the women she employed to nurse her 18 children. The Countess even speculated that the deaths of at least one, if not more, of her babies might have been directly attributable to the nurses' neglect.

Alice Thornton, whose vivid autobiography provides graphic detail about her childbearing years, also claimed to have nearly lost one child to the carelessness of its nurse. Thornton described how the nurse fell asleep while feeding and almost smothered the baby by 'overlaying' or rolling over on to it; fortunately the baby's grandmother noticed and rescued her.

Alice also subscribed to the common seventeenth century belief that bad milk could cause rickets and other illnesses, concluding that her daughter Betty had died when she was 18 months old, of rickets and consumption 'caused by ill milk at two nurses.' The fact that Daphne Lightfoot, the child's first nurse, fed Betty until she fell pregnant would have reinforced to Alice that Betty had not received the best milk. She also felt that the second nurse was not very capable, and she regretted not being able to keep as close an eye on Betty as she would have liked when the child was living at the nurse's house. The nurse lived over a mile away and Alice found this too far to walk or ride while she was heavily pregnant with her next child. This might seem a strange excuse, but Alice believed she had lost her first child at 32 weeks from walking a mile down a steep hill and so was understandably cautious.

When vicar Isaac Archer's wife Anne gave birth to her last child, Frances, in 1682, the baby was sent out to a wet-nurse, possibly because of the problems Anne had had with feeding after earlier deliveries. Sadly, Frances died shortly afterwards and Archer worried that the child had been over-lain, since the nurse was sleeping in a bed with three other people. After much soul searching, Archer decided his daughter's death was a punishment for his sins, including being short-tempered with his wife.

Despite the reservations of medics like Jane Sharp and the pleas of the Countess of Lincoln that women should acquiesce to God's will and nurse their own babies, the use of wet nurses appears to have risen during the seventeenth century. In 1695 Henry Newcome published a treatise similar to Elizabeth Clinton's, called *The Complete Mother, or an Earnest Persuasive to all Mothers (especially those of Rank or Quality) to Nurse their Own Children.* Newcome's argument closely resembles Clinton's, but Newcome also made it clear that if the husband absolutely refused to have his wife nurse his children, then her first duty was to obey him, 'and leave him to answer for the neglect, which she cannot help.'

The practice was so deeply embedded into society that it continued to the late 1800s. In the eighteenth century the ideas of Jean Jacques Rousseau promoted a model of family life quite unlike anything that had gone before, and encouraged maternal nursing. In the nineteenth century, concerns about hygiene and the rise of the formula product (invented in the 1860s) effectively ended the practice, since women who could not breastfeed had a viable and cheaper alternative.

Part IV

Women and Religion

Chapter Eleven

Religion and Worship
in Early Modern Women's Lives

In early modern England the majority of people believed in a Christian
God. Religious faith was a real, tangible part of people's day-to-day
lives. God was expected to be involved in all events, however large or
small, and signs of His favour or displeasure were keenly sought out. The
Church too, was an important part of daily life, but over the course of the
period (as previously touched on in the Introduction) the doctrine and form
of how people worshipped went through several drastic changes, and these
transitions all had a direct effect on women's lives.

Practising religion took both a private and a public form for early modern
people. The Protestant religions which developed during the Reformation
from the sixteenth century, encouraged the development of a personal
relationship with God, which was part of what promoted the publication of
the Bible in English, rather than the standard Latin, but, at the same time,
also put a woman's public performance of her religion very much on display.
In a sermon from 1635 Robert Shelford raged against women who, upon
entering church, before taking their 'pews, some make their courtesy in the
alley, but it is with their faces either toward their masters and mistresses,
or toward some of their betters in the parish.' For these women being seen
at church by their superiors was more important than the act of worship,
although, as Shelford reminded his reader, they should be focussing on God.

Wealthy women could also leave lasting proof of their piety by funding
monuments to be placed in their local church after their death. Often these
would take the form of statues depicting the woman and her husband in
prayer, or more modest inscribed plaques, such as one in St Martin's Church,
Exeter belonging to Elizabeth Butler who died in 1644. Elizabeth's wall
plaque states that she was so good a neighbour, mother, friend and wife that
Heaven insisted on reclaiming her. Women would also actively support the

church financially, even the impoverished: Ralph Josselin noted a donation he received from 'a poor maid' called Bridget in September 1647, who gave him 2 shillings and sixpence, a significant sum for her.

Just as God's presence was tangible to early modern people, so was that of Satan. The Puritan poet Anne Bradstreet discussed how, although she felt the presence of God, she had often been upset by the Devil tormenting her about the truth of scripture and asking her 'how I could know whether there was a God.' In a time before a clear understanding of mental illness, people also believed that Satan drove them to commit crimes such as suicide, an act that was illegal until 1961 and known as 'self-murder' in the early modern period. If someone was proven to have committed suicide, then all their estate would be confiscated by the State, since they were technically classed as a murderer, and the Church considered that deceased person's soul would be immediately consigned to hell.

The perceived presence of the Devil in daily life meant that in court trials, it was often reported that the defendant did not have 'God before her eyes' at the time of the crime, but was instead 'being moved and seduced by a devilish instigation.'

Reformation and Counter-reformation

The authorised state religion changed dramatically in the 1530s, when Henry VIII famously broke away from the Roman Catholic Church and installed himself as head of the newly formed Church of England. This new Church still consisted of all the elements of the Catholic faith, but with Henry as its head, not the Pope. The new state religion developed into Protestantism under the brief reign of Henry's heir Edward V. Henry's Catholic elder daughter, Mary I (1515–1568) instigated a counter-reformation, upon her accession to the throne, to return the country to Roman Catholicism. When Elizabeth I inherited the crown in 1558, she re-instated the Protestant religion, also including elements of Catholic doctrine.

What the ordinary woman made of all this turmoil is hard to ascertain. Certainly it must have been bewildering to see, during the late 1530s, the dismantling of institutions such as convents and monasteries. Hundreds of religious women were evicted, their churches whitewashed and elaborate ornamentation sent to the royal treasury. Yet, just years later they saw the altars (a sacred platform kept separate from the people who worshipped) reinstated with the ascent of Mary I to the throne, only to be removed again when Elizabeth succeeded her sister.

James IV of Scotland inherited the English throne from his second cousin in 1603, largely because he was also raised a Protestant. Under the reign of his son Charles I, there were fresh attempts to reinstate some of the pomp and splendour of Catholicism within the Church. This included the controversial restoration of altar rails, which provoked widespread unrest among the people, who saw such separation of God and his people as a step back towards Catholicism. In the women's ceremony of churching, the new Protestant religion banned new mothers from wearing veils, yet after the Restoration in 1660, a woman might be turned away from church if she failed to arrive wearing a veil.

One of the earliest women to be caught up in the turmoil of the Reformation was the Protestant reformer Anne Askew (1520–1546). Her case shows just how complicated the whole Reformation was, for despite the fact that most people associate it with Henry's divorce from Katherine of Aragon, it was about much more than that. Anne was tortured and burned at the stake for her beliefs several years after the Reformation began. Anne's Protestant views were considered seditious, as they went much further than the Henrician Church reforms. Although Henry had instated himself as the Head of the Church, he still considered the country Catholic and forbade the new Protestantism that was growing in Europe, inspired by the teachings of preachers such as Martin Luther.

Anne Askew was an extraordinary, unconventional woman, who for instance refused to take her husband's name on their marriage. She was married by arrangement to a conservative man from Lincolnshire, who threw her out of their home, unwilling to countenance her outspoken views. When she was arrested for preaching Protestant views, including refusing to believe in transubstantiation or that the bread in Holy Communion transformed into the body of Christ, in London the court ordered that Anne be sent home, but she was soon back in the city.

Anne was re-arrested and brutally tortured on the rack, possibly in an attempt to force her to implicate Queen Katherine Parr (1512–1548), who supported

Protestant reforms. Having confessed nothing, Anne was finally burned at the stake for heresy. She was only 25 when she died.

While accusations of heresy abounded in this turbulent times, only a very few women were burned at the stake for it. Baptist Joan Boucher was killed in this way in May 1550 for, amongst other things, being found guilty of distributing the forbidden Tyndale English translation of the Bible, despite not being able to read herself. Joan pointed out to her accusers that they had burned Anne Askew over a 'piece of bread,' but that they now believed in the same thing that Anne did.

One of those responsible for her conviction, John Rogers thought her punishment fitted the crime, but when Mary I began her reign, Rogers was the first to die in this way himself, showing the dangers of the changing State religions in the sixteenth century. Death by burning for heresy was practised very infrequently in the seventeenth century and was outlawed in the 1677 Ecclesiastical Jurisdiction Act, which limited the punishment for heresy to excommunication from the Church.

Religion and Daily Life

From the mid-sixteenth century onwards, in Elizabeth's reign, attendance at an Anglican church on Sundays was compulsory and non-attenders, known as recusants, were fined. This was partly motivated by the need, as Elizabeth saw it, to secure her throne and to keep Catholics down. She was ever fearful of reprisals from those factions still loyal to Mary, although some wealthy families chose to pay the fine rather than attend church.

The Church was not merely a place where worshippers heard sermons, it also marked the seasons and passage of the year with its various holy days; at Church courts people disputed all manner of minor incidents and crimes, such as sleights and slanders or sexual transgressions; and members of the congregation turned to their local minister for help with practical matters too. Ralph Josselin rode out to a nearby town in September 1646, to help sort out Goody Davies' struggles with a debtor. People also practised their religion at home. Children were taught the catechism and households would gather to hear passages from the Bible, which was published in English from the mid-sixteenth century and finally ordered into an official authorised edition by James I in 1611 (now known as the King James Bible).

Given the centrality of religion in people's lives, it is unsurprising that women and men interpreted all sorts of events in their lives as signs of God's favour or displeasure. Protestants who were literate were encouraged to keep a spiritual diary, which they could use to reflect on their relationship with God. Staunch Anglican Alice Thornton described how from childhood she had kept a record of 'what God had done for me.' Spiritual diaries might be kept private, but would often be shared with a minister.

Most people would routinely give thanks to God for any good fortune; this was not simply convention or an empty figure of speech, but part of a sincere belief system. A typical example of this sort of religious thinking can be seen when, after the death of her husband, Lady Joan Barrington had a crisis of faith. In 1629, her daughter Lady Elizabeth Masham wrote to comfort her mother, reminding her that all earthly upsets were essentially a 'means of the curing the great distemper of our souls, and may make us long for that home where all sorrows have an end and we shall triumph in joy and glory forever more.' Elizabeth was encouraging her mother to use adversity as a lesson in piety.

As Elizabeth Masham's advice to her mother suggests, women regularly analysed their relationship with God during periods of misfortune. Lady Elizabeth Mordaunt wrote about the miscarriages she had suffered, entitling her reflection, 'A thanksgiving after twice miscarrying, and a fever. March the 18th 1674.' Elizabeth changed these sad events into positive ones, interpreting her recovery from each miscarriage as a sign that God had been displeased with her but, by allowing her to recover, had agreed to give her a second chance: 'It is of the Lord's mercy that I was not consumed, but preserved through all these ills, and weaknesses (just punishments for my oft repeated transgressions).'

In the poetry she wrote shortly after a miscarriage, Lady Mary Carey also tried to turn the loss of a child into a positive religious experience. Lady Mary was married to George Payler at this time, but kept her previous married name, as was customary if the previous husband had been of a higher rank than his successor. She and her husband had written about their children in moving verse. In the poem 'Written by me at the Death of my 4th Son, & 5th Child Peregrine Payler,' created in May 1652, she described how, despite feeling like she had already given her all in childbearing, God had decided to send her one more baby.

Her last and most famous poem, 'Upon the Sight of my abortive Birth [*miscarriage*] the 31st of December 1657,' describes how she accepted God's will in taking away this baby to heaven, because God knew what it is like to lose a child himself and would not have done this lightly. She wrote that she would not grieve for her child in heaven, as it was now in the better place, and instead she would use the lesson to remember to value her two healthy children: 'By my dead, formless Babe teach me to prize: / My living, pretty Pair, Nat: & Bethia.' The poem concludes with the statement: 'And if herein God hath fulfilled his Will, / His Hand-Maid's pleased, completely happy still.'

Again, this was not merely poetic convention, but a valid way for Lady Mary to come to terms with her loss, and so a form of therapy. She made the same point in her life writing too, describing how:

> *I had tenderly loving Parents, good Husbands, the last is so, & good was it for me, that I was Wife to the first; God hath given me lovely Children, Sons, & Daughters, 5 in God's Bosom, 2 yet with me; 'tis best for me, & them, that those that died, died; 'tis best for me, & them, that those that live, live; many were the Mercies of them that died; & (in some kind) more are the Mercies of these that live, & all the Mercies of them both were my Mercies.*

God's hand was also seen when Alice Thornton became pregnant aged 41, in 1667. This was an unexpected pregnancy and after all she had been through in her previous confinements Alice was certainly not thrilled. The pregnancy was difficult and she grew weak and sickly. In her autobiography, she noted that: 'if it had been good in the eyes of my God, I should much rather (because of that) not to have been in this condition. But it is not a Christian's part to choose anything of this nature but what shall be the will of our heavenly father, be it never so contrary to our own desires.'

In contrast, Lady Mary Rich, Countess of Warwick, wrote in her autobiography of her intense desire to conceive another child after the death of her son and heir:

[a]*t my son's death I was not much more than thirty-eight years old, and therefore many, as well as my lord and myself, entertained some hopes of my having more children. But it pleased God to deny that great and desired blessing to us, and I cannot but acknowledge a just hand of God in not granting us our petition.*

She thought God was justified in refusing this request, however, because in the past, as a young wife she had deliberately chosen to have just two children. As she had conceived so easily, she was worried that she might have too many babies for the family to cope with financially, especially since she had gone against her father's wishes and married a younger son rather than a wealthy heir. She had also been concerned that because she 'childed so thick it would spoil my great vanity,' or, in other words, might have spoiled her figure.

Although Lady Mary didn't reveal the method she had used to limit her family, she mentioned that her husband had agreed with the decision at the time. Yet, now it had caused them to be without an heir, knowing that the situation was their own fault made 'our wound, in this case incurable, by letting our coal be quite put out,' meaning to have their hopes extinguished like a fire going out.

Similarly, Lady Margaret Hoby felt her infertility was a direct result of God's actions towards her, and so decided to demonstrate her piety by fasting for the day on 7 October 1603, in the hope that the Lord would grant 'that blessing which yet I want.' By demonstrating her submission to God's will through spending the day fasting and in prayer, Lady Margaret hoped to be blessed with a child, but this was not to be during any of her three marriages.

Religion and Health

In general, ill-health was taken as a sign of God's disfavour, for a healthy body and a healthy soul were seen as interdependent during this period. Hannah Allen wrote an account, published as *A Narrative of God's Gracious Dealings* in 1683, of the depressive illness she suffered, revealing that she interpreted it as a sign that she was out of favour with God. The bodily humour associated with melancholy or depression, black bile, was also known as the Devil's balm and was thought to dispose people towards sins such as self-harm.

In accordance with this belief, Brilliana Conway (later Lady Harley) paraphrased a section of William Perkins' *Cases of Conscience* (1606) in her 1622 commonplace book. She wrote that the Devil worked 'strange conceits' in believers' minds, sending 'to the brain and head fumes and mists which do corrupt the imagination and make the instrument of reason unfit for understanding Sins.'

In her early teenage years Hannah Allen had begun to suffer from poor health and she became more and more convinced that this was because she had committed an unpardonable sin. Blasphemy was cited in the Bible as the only sin God would not forgive and the thought that she might be guilty of this and so would go to Hell sent her into a deep despondency. In the depths of her despair she made attempts on her own life, including smoking spiders, which at this time were believed to be poisonous; locking herself under the floorboards; and re-opening wounds that a surgeon had made while letting her blood. This might sound unlikely to succeed to a modern reader and were perhaps more cries for help, but Hannah believed at the time that she was making serious attempts on her life at the Devil's instigation.

Hannah's story shows the very real effects that the perception of sin could have on the body and mind of a godly seventeenth century woman, and also how this could be mitigated, as Hannah sought help from physicians and ministers, using a combination of medical and spiritual cures.

When therapeutic treatments had beneficial results their efficacy was always explained as thanks to God's will. Lady Mary Rich went to Epsom and Tunbridge Wells to drink the iron-rich spa waters, in her grief after the death of her son, and noted how 'by the blessing of God I found a great deal of good in them.' After the birth of one of her children, Alice Thornton described how she continued to bleed for 20 weeks and became lame and weak. In August 1659, her doctor and her mother decided that she too should go to a spa town to recuperate, and so she was packed off to Scarborough with her husband. They stayed there for a month, 'in which time I did by the blessing of God recover my strength after the stay [*stopping*] of the former infirmity of bleeding, it leaving me within two days totally.'

Religion and Adolescence

It seems to have been quite common for girls to experience some sort of religious crisis as part of the turmoil and changes during adolescence. Hannah Allen's ill health and linked religious crisis started in her teens. Lady Dionys Fitzherbert (1580–c1640s) wrote about this sort of thing too, within a manuscript called 'An Anatomy for the Poor in Spirit.'

Lady Dionys' crisis manifested as an illness, which began suddenly while she was staying in the household of the dowager Countess of Huntingdon. She was embarrassed by the fact that she had not been sent money by her father to buy the customary New Year gifts exchanged by the wealthy, which, in particular, were used as a sign of respect to one's host. To get out of the celebrations, Dionys pretended to be ill, rather than face social embarrassment. However, that evening she became ill in reality, initially putting it down to a reaction from eating a baked apple. She described how, that 'night when I was sat by the fire one of my lady's women came to see me and gave me a baked apple, which I did eat, never thinking how ill it was for the disease I pretended to be troubled withal.'

Under the humoral system, eating fruit was often blamed for illnesses because of its wet properties, but in fact, although she didn't seem to realise it, cooked apples were thought to be therapeutic for invalids, so it is likely the maid was sent with a baked apple to help, rather than to catch her out, as she assumed.

Dionys' physical illness quickly escalated to a sort of mental breakdown initiated, it seems, by the guilt she felt. During this time her family believed her to be mad, and in her disturbed state she underwent a period of extreme anxiety about death and her religious faith, believing that she had become 'God's enemy.' At one stage she became convinced that she was being taken on a trip to Oxford to be put to death by burning, the traditional death of witches and heretics. Quite often, she contemplated suicide, considering throwing herself into a river on her journey home to Wales, and only stopping herself because it would be a sin against God.

After a period at home, Dionys soon recovered. In common with Lady Elizabeth Delaval, Dionys subsequently resolved to change her manner of living to become more pious and rise earlier (at 3 or 4 am) to pray and read scripture, and to limit herself to two meals a day. However her recovery was not a straightforward process and she described many occasions when she was weak and tearful, because she thought the Devil was still tempting her into sin.

Religion and Providence

The outbreaks of serious calamities, such as the recurrent plague epidemics, or isolated disasters, like the Great Fire of London in 1666, were often analysed to try to uncover what God had meant people to learn from them. News of the Great Fire in London made it into Alice Thornton's autobiography, where she noted that 'about the 2nd of September 1666 began the great fire in London, which in 4 days consumed 13200 houses, 89 churches, and without the miraculous Providence of God it had devoured the whole city.' Significantly, while she recorded the facts about the fire, she gave God and divine providence the credit for not making the damage any worse.

Events surrounding the 1642–1651 Civil Wars and the execution of Charles I in 1649 were interpreted by both sides of the political divide for signs of God's will. Some thought the Civil Wars were punishment for the sins of the English people for not reforming the Church enough, or for changing it too much. In response to such calamities, the Church ordered an increase in feast or fasting days. A feast day was a religious anniversary observed with rejoicing, whereas a fast day was characterised by abstinence, where the population would deny themselves food and abstain from sexual intercourse in order to become closer to God.

A table detailing which days were designated as occasions for feasting or fasting was given in the *Book of Common Prayer*, but Parliament or the monarch could appoint additional fast days to pray for issues of national importance and set prayers were read in congregations around the country. Individual communities also held their own fast days to pray or give thanks, perhaps for the recovery of individual members of the congregation or for the health of the collective group after an epidemic.

Lady Elizabeth Delaval reflected on how, during the great plague outbreak of 1665 she was appalled that more people weren't urgently reflecting on the danger the country was in: ''Tis wonderful and indeed strikes one with horror to behold that this increase of the raging pestilence has no effect upon us.' Another gentlewoman, Lady Elizabeth Mordaunt also prayed for guidance about this plague outbreak and, after praying on behalf of the whole nation, and her family in particular, she asked God for help: 'Dearest Lord direct and guide my dear husband and me, what we shall do, where we shall abide, that in all things we may do thy will, and in what place soever we be, dearest Lord protect both us and ours either abroad or at home.'

From the mid-sixteenth century to the reign of Queen Anne in the early eighteenth century, the formalities of religious worship changed many times. What was meant by the now familiar definitions of Protestant and Catholic was disputed and considerably altered, but a belief in God and visible worship, combined with private reflections played a part in most women's daily lives throughout this time. Similarly, most women probably took the view that the best option was to accept publicly whatever religious practices the State was enforcing at any given time, whatever her private view about these upheavals was.

The ordering of the calendar and the seasons defined by the Church calendar reinforced the centrality and naturalness of faith in people's lives, as did the framework by which women could turn to God as the natural explanation for tragedies such as bereavements and illnesses. The surety of a faith in God clearly provided comfort to women in trying as well as happier times.

Chapter Twelve

Prophetesses and Preachers:
Non-conformist Women

While the previous chapter has shown that the majority of women worshipped peacefully in the forms the State sanctioned, this was far from the case for all women. Part of the teaching of the new Protestant faith which gradually developed over the decades of the Reformation from the sixteenth century, was to encourage believers to question religion. By the seventeenth century, the established State religion was Anglican but many people felt increasingly dissatisfied with the practices it involved. This gave rise to a number of groups or sects, which formed breakaway or nonconformist religions.

Women were represented within all these groups. From within Protestantism grew Puritanism, whose members saw their worship as purer and more Biblically based than State Protestantism. At various times these religious groups were tolerated by the State, at others they were persecuted. The English Civil Wars of the 1640s were partly brought about by the religious differences which emerged in the preceding decades and famously Oliver Cromwell (1599–1658), as Lord Protector from 1653, helped to establish a Puritan regime. Despite this, during the Interregnum (the 11 years during which England was a commonwealth) various religious sects co-existed peacefully, with Cromwell only prosecuting those he perceived as a threat to the stability of his regime, such as the Quakers.

When Charles II was instated in 1660, he vowed that he would be tolerant towards the minority Protestant religions, but he reneged on this promise almost immediately. In 1662 his Parliament introduced a set of laws, known as the Clarendon Code, against those that did not conform to the Established Church, and until his Catholic brother James II was removed from the throne during the Glorious Revolution of 1688, so-called nonconformists, including Independents, Presbyterians, Baptists, Quakers, and Catholics, experienced varying levels of persecution.

After James fled the country and was assumed to have abdicated, his son-in-law (also his nephew) and his elder daughter, William and Mary, ascended, as joint rulers, to the English throne, the Act of Toleration was passed, granting religious freedoms to all non-conformist groups, except Catholics and atheists.

The majority of the population went along with the Established Church, but these dissenting groups were a vocal minority, especially in the mid-seventeenth century. These religions were particularly attractive to women, in part because they were rare public forums where women could have a voice. While the official religion upheld the message in 1 Corinthians 14: 34-35, which begins 'let your women keep silent in the churches,' and while the issue still occupied many theologians, the dissenting sects were often founded on the principle of all participants, both male and female, giving testimony of God's presence in their lives. Quakerism, in particular, had women-only meetings which provided a safe space for women to worship.

In the rest of this chapter, the main religious divisions throughout this period and some examples of the women who identified with minority religious groups, or even simply wrote about them, will be explored.

Catholicism

The Anglican Church was still not fully secure when James I came to the throne, despite Elizabeth I's long Protestant reign. Fears of a Catholic resurgence were never far away throughout the seventeenth century, as some of the most tumultuous events of the period – from the Gunpowder Plot of 1605 to the Glorious Revolution of 1688 – demonstrate. James I inherited Elizabeth's throne, in part, because he had been raised a Protestant, yet his wife, Anne of Denmark, was thought to have converted to Catholicism around 1600, just before he acceded to the throne.

Many at the Stuart court had Catholic connections or sympathies and, indeed, a number of courtiers disguised their true faith. James' heir, Charles I, was married to the Catholic Henrietta Maria, and their son Charles II, himself married to a Catholic, was also suspected by some to be a convert, while his brother and heir James II's open Catholicism led to his abdication.

Women played a key role in upholding the 'old faith,' as Catholicism was known. In the 1590s Henry Ferrers, an underground Catholic, rented his manor house at Baddesley Clinton in the Midlands to Anne Vaux (1562–1637), who used it as a safe house for Catholic priests. Anne was known as a feisty and vocal woman, one who would probably have become a nun had not the Reformation and Dissolution of the Monasteries removed this option for young women, unless they had the means and were willing to move abroad to a Catholic country. The Catholic faith valued virginity and celibacy in a way that the Established Church did not, and instead of becoming a nun, Anne decided to remain single and devote her life to funding a secret network of Jesuit priests who were clandestinely travelling to England from France.

By arguing that she had no intention of marrying, Anne successfully sued her guardian Sir Thomas Tresham in the Court of Wards. As an orphan from a higher-ranking family, her guardianship was the responsibility of the Court. The assets and responsibility for wards of court were sold to the highest bidder, since they could often make money from managing (or mismanaging) this wealth until the orphan came of age. However, in Anne's case, by successfully gaining access to her marriage portion (the money that was intended to form her dowry) she could live independently. Armed with the cash, Anne had three ingenious priest holes built into her manor house, in which an illegal priest could hide if the authorities received a tip-off that he was in the area.

The Jesuit priests risked their lives to come to England to perform mass for Catholic families. Anne's involvement in underground Catholic networks did not go unnoticed, and she was arrested after the Gunpowder Plot but soon released. At Coughton Court, another large property in the Midlands containing priest holes, owned by Thomas Throckmorton, brother-in-law of Sir Thomas Tresham, masses could be performed in relative safety, due to the design of the building.

Anne Vaux's guardian Sir Thomas was famous for his recusancy, or failure to attend Anglican services. As recusants were merely fined for non-attendance, effectively an additional tax upon openly Catholic households, but many underground Catholics attended church services to avoid being noticed. Lady Elizabeth Delaval wrote a meditation on the sight of a 'very poor old man at church who was a Roman Catholic,' in the 1660s. She revealed that the sight of a man going to church merely to save money made her weep. Typically, Elizabeth used the incident to reflect upon her own sins, in this case because while the old man was deaf and confused and had an excuse for failing to pay attention, she had wilfully daydreamed during some parts of the service.

Helen More (1606–1633), the great-great-granddaughter of Henry VIII's martyred chancellor Sir Thomas More, left England to move to France, where she became a nun at the Our Lady of Comfort convent, in Cambrai. There she became one of the founders of a Benedictine order at Stanbrook Abbey in 1625. From the convent Helen More wrote devotional books, which were posthumously published in 1657, under her chosen religious name of Gertrude More. One of these texts, *The Holy Practises of a Divine Lover*, uses the Catholic concept of a nun choosing to become the bride of Christ, rather than having an earthly husband.

The loss of the chance to live in retirement as a nun in England was something that other young Catholic women felt keenly. When she lost her only son shortly after being widowed, Gertrude Thimelby (1617–1668), like Gertrude More, chose to enter a convent. Thimelby was a member of the close-knit Aston and Thimelby Catholic families of Lincolnshire, but after her bereavements she went to live in St Monica's nunnery in Louvain, where her sister-in-law was the abbess. She lived there until her death.

Puritans and Pilgrims

While there were perennial concerns about a potential resurgence of Catholicism, which would have destabilised the country in the seventeenth century, as the Reformation and Counter-reformations of the previous century had at the same time, many people who adhered to the new Protestant faith believed that the Reformation had not gone far enough. People who believed in striving for a more direct, purer relationship with God, which cut out the need for priests and what they saw as superstitious practices, such as relics, became known as Puritans, an umbrella term which was often used in a derogatory sense.

In common with many of the various non-conformist Protestants, Puritans saw anything that was not specifically ordered in the Bible as superstition and ungodly. For instance, they often did not believe in infant baptism, the exchanging of wedding rings and the celebration of significant holy days like Christmas and Easter with the traditional feasts and revelling. Another key tenet among these religions was a belief in sixteenth century theologian John Calvin's idea of predestination. This theory stated that whether or not you were one of God's chosen people was determined before your birth, and believers spent a great deal of time examining signs and events in their lives for clues as to whether they were saved or damned. Hannah Allen took her belief that she had committed an unpardonable sin to be a sign that she was predestined for damnation, developing a profound spiritual melancholy at the thought.

A popular way of examining signs to discover your fate after death was making anagrams from the letters in your name. Lady Dionys Fitzherbert did this during her religious breakdown and she decided that the various combinations of her name all proved unequivocally that she was 'an adversary of God.' When she recovered, Dionys blamed Satan for these strange constructions and dismissed them. Another Puritan, Elizabeth Major (b. 1628), also made an anagram from her name to prove she was in the elect, coming up with the phrase 'O I am a blest Heir,' which she used in the title of a poem expressing her conviction that she was an heir of the kingdom of God.

Protestants had been encouraged in 1558 when, on inheriting the throne, the Protestant Elizabeth I oversaw the Act of Uniformity, which reinstated her father's break from the Church of Rome. As previously referred to, this act also required people to attend church services from the English Book of Common Prayer. However, the following year, some of the requirements of the Act were moderated in the Act Settlement of 1559, among them the requirement for priests to wear robes. This meant that some felt that the break from Rome was being undermined.

Charles I's decision to appoint William Laud as Archbishop of London enhanced the graving rift between Puritans and the Established Church. Laud wanted to incorporate features such as altar rails back into services, which Puritans saw as too closely aligned to Catholic practices. In 1630, frustrated by the lack of progress within the Established Church, a number of like-minded English Puritans emigrated to the New World to be free to worship as they saw fit, away from the Laudian reforms and mounting political tensions.

Two of the dowager Countess of Lincoln's daughters were amongst those who joined the Great Migration to America. A fleet of 11 ships, including a flagship *Arbella*, named after one of the Clinton sisters, Lady Arabella Johnson (1595–1630), departed in the spring of that year. Like many who struggled to adapt to the privations of settler life, Arabella died a few months later, in Salem, Massachusetts.

Also on board was teenager Anne Bradstreet, who went on to become America's first published poet. Bradsteet's father Thomas Dudley had worked as a steward for Theophilus Clinton, Earl of Lincoln, and both men were staunchly Puritan. This link gave Dudley the chance to have his daughter educated as a gentlewoman within the Clinton family. The Dudley family gained their place on board the ship, because John Humphrey who was married to Lady Susan Clinton (1602–c1650) couldn't go in the first wave (he and his wife would briefly join the colony in 1634).

Presbyterians

The origins of Presbyterianism stem from the Reformation, but during the build up to the English Civil Wars a particularly significant kind of English Presbyterianism was established. Presbyterians believed in the reformation of the Church (their name stems from the Latin term for 'church') but were still loyal to the crown, and so against the execution of Charles I.

Despite their support for the crown, after the Restoration Presbyterians were persecuted because their ministers were unable to sign the new 1662 Act of Uniformity of Public Prayer. This Act required ministers to only preach from the Book of Common Prayer and administer the rites and sacraments of the Established Church. It led to 2,000 ministers losing their posts in a 'the Great Expulsion.' Before this Act came into force Presbyterians had seen themselves as an inclusive religion within the Anglican faith, rather than as a separate faction, yet Presbyterians were now vilified in the press.

Lady Elizabeth Delaval, who was a committed Anglican, tells an anecdote in her book of meditations which displays some of the stereotypes about the nature of Presbyterians. In it a trusted servant of her aunt Lady Stanhope, attempted to convert her to Presbyterianism. Elizabeth wrote that:

> *Mistress Carter begun most perniciously to insinuate Presbyterian principles into me, in some intervals of time when she did not talk to me of love and fairy tales; so that had I not been delivered soon out of her hands without doubt I should have had the great misfortune of being bred up a Presbyterian, for at the time of my life she could have turned me which way she pleased, as easily as she might have bowed a tender twig.*

Elizabeth subsequently formed a friendship with Miss Corny an Anglican minister's daughter; Corny, she felt, was a friend 'sent me by God' at a time of need, when she was still very upset by the actions of Carter.

Separatists, Particular Baptists, and Fifth Monarchists

While the Puritan faith saw itself as part of the state religion in that it was Anglican but preferred to be led by the Bible and not to perform any rites or rituals not set out in the text, independents or separatists set themselves apart and only admitted new members to their congregations following an oral presentation of their relationship with God and a vote amongst existing members. These groups were also called 'gathered churches' and within this definition were a number of independent churches, all with slightly different beliefs.

These churches could treat their members harshly. A flurry of pamphlets appeared in response to one incident during the mid-seventeenth century, when Susanna Parr (*fl.* 1650–1659) and Mary Allein were excommunicated from their gathered church of Christ in Exeter in 1657. The women seem to have been excluded on the grounds that they had looked around other churches to see if they found the preaching more agreeable, although their church officials denied this. The official charge was that they had behaved in a disorderly manner in other churches.

Mary Allein seems to have regretted leaving the church where all her children had been baptised and decided to go to visit her brother-in-law in Taunton to seek his advice. When the trip was delayed Mary caused more scandal by going off on her own with her midwife, leaving her husband and children behind, even though she was heavily pregnant. Obviously, there was some urgency on her part, since the child's baptism was at stake, and her own lying-in would have prevented travel afterwards for a number of weeks. Her baby Susanna, no doubt named after her friend, was born in November 1657, while she was away. The child was baptised in Taunton much to her husband's dismay.

The practice of adult baptism developed during the early seventeenth century, founded on the principle that baptising infants was not a scriptural practice and that, instead, it should be undertaken by professing adults, who would be fully immersed in a river or stream. The issue of infant baptism caused much consternation in the period not just amongst theologians and clergy but lay people too. Ralph Josselin recorded many arguments and debates he had on the topic. Even husbands and wives with conflicting views fell out about this matter, though few took the issue as seriously as John and Mary Champian, who became the subject of a pamphlet. In *Bloody News from Dover* (1646), the writer described how, as a Presbyterian, John Champian wanted to have their child baptised but his Baptist wife did not. When John returned from work one day he found that Mary had chopped the baby's head off to prevent him from baptising it. The pamphleteer concluded that Mary Champian had been seduced by the Devil.

The writer and minister, John Bunyan, author of *Pilgrim's Progress* (1678) is probably the most famous figure associated with the seventeenth century Baptists. Agnes Beaumont became a follower of Bunyan after hearing him preach. In her description of her religious conversion, published long after her death, Agnes discusses the troubles her religious beliefs caused her. Agnes' family had also been to listen to Bunyan preach, but her father was turned against him by some villagers.

In her narrative of the events of 1674, Agnes described how her father had only allowed her to go to hear Bunyan preach providing she got a lift to the church at Gamlingay on family friend, John Wilson's horse. When Wilson failed to arrive, instead she rode on the back of Bunyan's horse, after he serendipitously turned up at her brother's farm. Agnes' father was furious when he heard this, and tried to chase after Bunyan's horse. When Agnes arrived home later that day, unaware of the trouble she had caused, she was cold and dirty but her father refused her entry to the house, saying that she should stay at night where she had stayed all day.

After spending a cold night in the barn, Agnes tried once more with her father. He was still angry and turned her away, ignoring her plea that he might at least let her collect her Bible and pattens. He refused and said she wouldn't get another penny from him. Before they could be reconciled Agnes' father died, and this caused villagers, including the village priest Mr Lane and lawyer Mr Freery, to claim that Agnes had poisoned him. If found guilty of this charge, Agnes would have faced death by burning for petty treason, the crime of killing a husband or father, and punishable by burning at the stake, but the inquest into his death concluded that he had died of natural causes.

As part of her public vindication, Agnes' book quotes her father's dying words in which, she claimed, he spoke regretfully of his harsh behaviour towards her, saying 'I have been Against you for seeking after Jesus Christ; the Lord forgive me, and lay not that sin to my Charge.' However the terror of being thought guilty of murder must have been very real, as in her account Agnes likens herself to biblical figures who bore their trials with dignity.

Prophetess Anne Wentworth (1630–1693) had a completely opposing experience to Agnes, but she also took up her pen to write about her religious persecution, in Anne's case by the Baptist church. In an earlier pamphlet, *A True Account of Anne Wentworth* (1679), Anne described how she had been unhappily married for 18 years: 'after 18 years I had been my Husband's wife, and was consumed to skin and bone, a forlorn sad spectacle to be seen, unlike a woman; for my days had been spent with sighing, and my years with crying.'

Anne Wentworth is vague about the exact nature of her suffering, but in her next work, *England's Spiritual Pill* (1679), she referred to her husband as being verbally abusive and cruel. Anne saw her husband and the Baptist church where they worshipped as interconnected, and described how her body and soul both began to recover after God told her to leave the church.

People often treated dissenters with suspicion, and Ralph Josselin recorded a story he had heard about the arrest and imprisonment of an Anabaptist, who 're-baptised' a woman who died immediately afterwards. Complete submersion in water was thought to be unhealthy anyway, which added to general distrust of adult baptism, and many also suspected the motives of men and women involved in this activity and thought it might lead to sexual activity.

Fifth Monarchists

The Fifth Monarchists or Millenarianists were a short-lived sect which briefly flourished in the 1650s. They were one of a number of so-called dissenting groups, along with other sects known as Muggletons, Levellers, Diggers, and the Ranters, for example. These factions were organised to greater or lesser degrees, with some just generic names given to individuals who expressed similar ideas.

The Fifth Monarchists took their name from a prediction in the Bible, which stated that there had been four kingdoms (Babylonian, Persian, Macedonian, and Roman), and the fifth and final one, the Kingdom of Christ, was imminent. This rule would last for a thousand years and end only at judgement day. Fifth Monarchists viewed the execution of Charles I and the turmoil of the Civil Wars as precursors to the end of the world. Anna Trapnel (*fl.*1642–1660), a Baptist and Fifth Monarchist, claimed to be a prophet and would sing in a trance-like state. To profess usually meant to communicate the word of God at this time, not to make predictions, although she did this too, predicting Cromwell's defeat of the Scots and the Dutch.

Initially, Anna was a big supporter of Cromwell and the Commonwealth, but after Cromwell declared himself Lord Protector on 16 December 1653 (an event she also claimed to have predicted), she felt unable to support him any longer. Fifth Monarchists believed in the idea of the lowly and dispossessed inheriting the earth, and she thought Cromwell had neglected this cause, becoming in her eyes the 'antichrist.'

Anna went into her first trance-like state while at Whitehall, listening to the sedition proceedings against preacher Vavasor Powell. She was taken to a nearby tavern, where she lay on a bed raving for 11 days and 12 nights, with her words being carefully copied down by a scribe. The result was *The Cry of Stone*, published in 1654, a book written partly in prose and partly in verse. In it, she included the following words about Cromwell:

Must thy servant that is now upon the throne, must he now die and go out like
a candle? Oh that thy servant could mourn day and night for him. Oh that he
might be recovered out of that vainglorious council, out of their traps and gins!

Anna and other Fifth Monarchists felt that Cromwell had fallen into the same
trappings as the former king and had effectively sold out, thus failing to keep his
word. They opposed his adoption of the title 'Protector,' making him king in all
but name (in fact Cromwell was to be offered the title of King in 1657, but he
refused it). As a result of her book, Anna became something of a celebrity and
was therefore viewed as dangerous by the protectorate. She was duly arrested
and accused of 'witchcraft, madness, whoredom, vagrancy, and seditious intent.'
Her defence made clear that, as a single woman, she was free to behave as she
liked, including travelling and publishing books. She essentially claimed that as
an unmarried woman and a taxpayer she had the same rights as any man.

Not everyone was impressed by the prophetess and an anonymously
authored book, *Christianity No Enthusiasm* (1678) discussed sensationalised
stories about Anna, linking her to the Quakers, its real target. In a letter to the
reader, the author stated: 'Anna Trapnel exceeds both the Quakers and most
of the other Pretenders, in excessive fastings, Poetical Enthusiasms, lucky
hits upon several things that came to pass afterwards, rapturous Devotions.'
Anna's predictions are presented as lucky guesses. The English successes in
the Dutch war, one of her accurate predictions, was of particular interest to her,
the author revealed, because lots of her fellow Fifth Monarchists were in the
cloth trade and in competition with the Dutch. A war suited them financially
and they also saw it is a divine crusade, because the Dutch had supported the
deposed house of Stuart. After the Restoration one of their leaders, Major-
General Thomas Harrison was the first regicide (or signatory to the death
warrant of Charles I) to be executed. A brief uprising led by Thomas Venner,
resulted in a group of Fifth Monarchists being executed for high treason, and
after 1661 the group was no longer active.

The Society of Friends or the Quakers

The Society of Friends became known as Quakers after the founder of the
religion, George Fox (1624–1691), told a magistrate that he should 'quake

or tremble in the sight of God.' While it was originally intended to mock believers, the name stuck. Quakerism was established in the 1650s, built upon the idea that by keeping silent you would be able to sense the presence of God, the 'inner light' which would guide you. The presence of the inner-light could cause worshippers to enter an ecstatic, trance-like state. The idea of an inner-light removed the perceived need for a hierarchy and structure to worship so prevalent in other religions. For this reason it was seen as potentially dangerous by those in authority.

Quakerism was co-founded by Margaret Fell (1614–1702) whose home in Swarthmore became an important meeting place for early Quakers. As result of this, she spent around a year in prison for breaking the Conventicle Act of 1664, one of the Clarendon Code laws which forbade meetings of more than five people outside services within the Established Church. Margaret married George Fox in the late 1660s after the death of her first husband. Both spent periods in gaol for their beliefs and specifically for their refusal to swear oaths, and were frequently apart while he preached in London and overseas.

Margaret published a number of books on topics associated with her beliefs, and under her influence, the Quakers held regular monthly meetings for women only. In his eulogy to his step-daughter Sarah Featherstone, Thomas Brown noted how at these meetings Sarah would contribute with all her might, and help the poor 'Friends' who struggled financially, taking eggs to a local widow, for example.

Another Quaker woman, Martha Simmons (1624–1665) wrote a number of books on her faith in the 1650s, but in 1655 she was imprisoned several times for attention-grabbing acts, such as walking through towns in sackcloth and ashes. Like other Quakers, both male and female, Simmons was reported to walk the streets naked to demonstrate her spiritual innocence in contrast to the rest of society. It is important to mention that in early modern times nudity could also mean being stripped down to the shift or under-dress, rather than entirely unclothed. In the summer of 1656, Simmons' activism and, in particular, her practice of interrupting male speakers in meetings, shouting 'innocency' led to her being accused of witchcraft, implicated by those within her own religion, including George Fox.

Just as much of what is known about the experience of attending gathered churches comes from women's conversion narratives, so too in her autobiography, Mary Penington (1623–1682) described how she converted to Quakerism. Her interest in religion was piqued when, as a teenager in 1637, she heard the story of how Puritan William Prynne, along with Henry Burton and John Bastwick, was summoned before the Star Chamber (a unique court which operated under the monarch from medieval times until 1641 and was made up largely of privy councillors) and charged with sedition for publishing anti-establishment pamphlets. The three men were found guilty and sentenced, amongst other punishments, to have their ears cropped; having already had them trimmed once before, Prynne was now set to lose the remainder of his ears. This event made a significant impression on the teenage Mary Proude, as she recorded it as a formative episode in her religious development.

Subsequently, when Mary had the chance to hear a Puritan minister preach she came increasingly to believe that this was the true way to worship. At 18, Mary married the like-minded Sir William Springett, without 'the use of a ring,' believing it to be another superstition of the Established Church. Springett died while Mary was pregnant with their only child, a daughter Gulielma Maria, named after her father. Carrying on the precedent they had set together of rejecting hymn singing and Holy Communion, Mary faced the ire of friends and family for refusing to have her daughter baptised.

Following her husband's death, Mary had a period of religious doubt and began going to dances, playing cards, indulging in fine foods, and wearing high fashions. Becoming disillusioned with this frivolous life, Mary had a dream in which Christ appeared to her as a 'fresh lovely youth, clad in gray cloth, very plain and neat,' and shortly afterwards she married the author Isaac Penington. The couple were formally accepted into the Quakers in 1656, following a friendship with George Fox.

However, their newly adopted Quakerism caused Mary to be alienated from much of society, and their refusal to swear an oath led to the Peningtons losing several court cases, with the loss of land and money. After Isaac's death, Mary wrote a testimony vindicating her husband's character in a posthumous collection of his works, as his reputation was repeatedly attacked because of his faith. Mary's story demonstrates that the decision to join a breakaway religion could not be taken lightly. Sarah Featherstone Brown recorded in a tribute to her late daughter, also Sarah, who died aged 15, how the family would be accosted on their way to their meetings, with people jeering 'rogue' and 'whore' at them.

As these accounts show, women had central and meaningful roles within all the nonconformist religions. What comes across time and again is the bravery of the women who participated. Whether hiding Jesuit priests or of professing their beliefs in public, these women took significant personal risks, showing just how important their beliefs were to them.

Part V

Women in Public Life

Chapter Thirteen

Courts and Criminals

E arly modern England was a highly litigious place. People were continually suing each other, even for quite small things, such as a passing insult, and most of these minor disputes played out in the Church Courts. Londoners used the phrase 'going to Paul's' to refer to taking someone to the court at St Paul's Cathedral.

Throughout the country too, local churches held ecclesiastic courts, which were mainly concerned with the moral behaviour of parishioners and so became known as 'bawdy courts.' In 1613, Suzannah Hall, the elder daughter of William Shakespeare, sued John Lane for slander in church court, after he said that she was suffering from 'running of the reins' (implying a sexually transmitted disease), having been 'naughty' with a Rafe Smith. Lane didn't turn up to defend himself and was duly excommunicated from the church, leaving Suzannah exonerated.

In other church court trials officiated over by church wardens and similar authority figures then, punishments could take the archaic form of the ducking or cucking stool and the scold's bridle. The cucking stool was a raised highchair in which a woman found guilty of scolding, nagging or of other unseemly conduct might be strapped into and paraded round the town; its more sinister variation, the ducking stool, saw women plunged in to a pond or river repeatedly, at risk of death from drowning or shock. Dishonest tradesmen were occasionally subjected to this punishment too.

The scold's bridle, however, seems to have been a punishment that applied exclusively to women. It is mentioned within a deposition cited in *England's Grievance Discovered* (1655), a text on the coal trade and the harsh treatment of northern workers by magistrates. Ralph Gardiner described how a John Willis of Ipswich swore on oath that in Newcastle, he had seen 'one Ann Bidlestone drove through the streets by an Officer,' tied to a rope, 'the other end fastened to an Engine called the Branks, which is like a Crown, it being of Iron, which was muzzled over the head and face, with a great gap or tongue of Iron forced into her mouth, which forced the blood out.' This torture was meted out for 'chiding, and scolding women,' and Willis swore he had seen it done often to others.

In addition to the ecclesiastical courts, the local magistrates courts were held at regular intervals in all major towns throughout the country, presided over by local Justices of the Peace. The more serious cases were referred to the Courts of Assizes (which would become the Crown Courts in the 1970s) to be heard in front of a High Court Judge. In London, the most serious cases were tried at the Central Criminal Court, known locally as the Old Bailey. This chapter takes a look at some of the criminal cases which ended up at London's Criminal Court, and the women perpetrators at the centre of them.

The trial transcripts from this particular court between 1674 and 1913 have been digitised and made available online at *The Proceedings of the Old Bailey* (*oldbaileyonline.org*), which makes their records uniquely accessible. In the seventeenth century, capital punishment could be ordered for an array of crimes, including grand larceny, the theft of any items valued at over a shilling – hence the phrase you might as well be hanged for a sheep as a lamb. Theft of goods valued under 12 pence was considered petty larceny, for which the punishment for both sexes could include being stripped to the waist and whipped in public.

However gruesome this seems, it was better than being hanged for grand larceny and so juries would sometimes undervalue the cost of stolen goods to ensure that a guilty verdict would not result in the defendant's death. This happened in June 1677, in the case of an unnamed young girl convicted of stealing 3 ounces of silver plate; she claimed to have been encouraged in her crimes by two apple-selling women. The plate was deliberately valued by the jury at 10 pence, so the girl was sentenced to be whipped. The court recorder commented that the two apple-sellers should also be tried and given more severe punishments for leading the child astray.

For first convictions of some serious crimes it was possible for men to claim 'the benefit of the clergy.' According to this custom, if they could read a passage from the Bible, then they would be handed over to the church to be dealt with, rather than the courts. The crimes of murder and rape, amongst others, were not eligible for this exemption but a murder trial could bring in a conviction for manslaughter which was eligible for the exemption, meaning a defendant could be let off. As it was a well-known loophole, not only clergymen claimed this right. Any literate man convicted of a crime could try it, as in the famous case of the playwright and poet Ben Jonson, who was convicted of manslaughter in 1598.

From 1623 women were also granted the right to claim benefit of the clergy and given the opportunity to read from the fifty-first psalm, but only in cases of petty larceny. From the 1690s, women were allowed to claim the benefit on the same basis as men. This one-off exemption would result in the prisoner's sentence being commuted to branding on the thumb, to ensure they could not make the same claim in future: M for a manslaughter or F for a felony.

Women sentenced to death could also claim a stay of execution by claiming to be pregnant. If, upon examination by a panel of experienced matrons, the woman was found to be pregnant, her sentence might be commuted or, usually, simply deferred until after the birth. Crucially, the pregnancy had to be beyond the stage of quickening, where the child had moved in the womb and so was considered to be a living being with a soul. Often, after the baby was born, the mother would receive a pardon on account of her child. However, as for men, sometimes a death sentence would merely be commuted to transportation at the plea of the defendant.

As has been demonstrated repeatedly in this book, religion and belief in God lay at the heart of early modern English society. A recurrent claim in the records of court cases is that the defendant did not have 'God before her eyes' at the time of the crime, but was instead 'moved and seduced by a devilish instigation.' This claim now sounds extravagant, but it would have been entirely unremarkable to contemporaries.

Petty Treason

One crime that invariably resulted in the death sentence was if a woman should murder her husband. This was known as 'petty treason,' because her husband was considered the woman's master, just as the king was master of the nation and a crime against him was considered treason, so was crime against one's husband, albeit a more minor form. The punishment for petty treason was death by burning.

One woman convicted of this crime was Elizabeth Lylliman in July 1675. On the day of her trial Elizabeth was the only prisoner ordered to be 'burned to ashes.' The scene leading up to her crime is one of apparent domesticity. The Lyllimans had lived in Goodmans Fields, in central London. On the evening of his death, Mr Lylliman had bought a piece of dried mackerel for his supper and borrowed a knife from a cobbler, who kept a stall outside their house, to prepare the fish. While the fish was bubbling on the fire, Elizabeth stabbed her husband through the heart with the borrowed knife. As he was dying, he called out to the tradesman who testified that Mr Lylliman repeatedly named his wife as his assailant; this evidence was accepted by the court and resulted in Elizabeth Lylliman's conviction, despite her denials.

In another case of petty treason, a French woman, Mary Aubry, aged about 50, pleaded guilty in February 1688 to strangling her husband Dennis with her garter. The trial had to be conducted using an interpreter, but it quickly became clear that Mary had been unhappy for some time and had said repeatedly that she would kill her husband one day. Dennis had come home at 5am that morning, extremely drunk, and Mary took the opportunity to murder him. After his death, Mary was left with the problem of how to dispose of the body. She ran to get her son, who was employed as a servant to a Mr Dubois.

Her son helped her to cut up and throw the body of his step-father (referred to in court in his father-in-law, the usual seventeenth century name for a step-parent) in the communal privy. The court record describes how, 'she cut off the legs and arms, and threw them into the Savoy house-of-office, as also the thighs, and carried the trunk of the body, laying it in a common place in Parker's Lane, wrapping the head also in a cloth, and flinging it in a house of office.'

When the body was found, Dennis Aubry was soon identified by a mark on his hand and his wife confessed. Despite her guilty plea, Mary was sentenced to death by burning, but her son and several other men who were tried for aiding and abetting her were either bound over for good behaviour or acquitted outright. The transcription simply records that the sentence was handed down, not what happened next.

Infanticide and Concealing a Birth

Another crime for which women were tried was infanticide, killing an infant aged under 12 months, which became a capital offence in 1624. The records of the Old Bailey show that 135 such cases were brought between 1674 and 1740, roughly two a year in the Greater London area. The women brought to trial were often treated sympathetically, which perhaps contradicts many people's perceptions of the period.

Married women were much less likely to be convicted of infanticide than single women. In one particularly distressing case from January 1675 a woman from St Martin in the Fields, who retained her anonymity in the court records, was acquitted despite having killed her newborn by throwing it in the fire. Even though the woman had arranged to have the baby's nurse sent out on errands to afford her the time to murder the baby, the jury recorded a not guilty verdict, due to the woman being considered not to have been of sound mind at the time.

Claims of being 'distracted' or not of sound mind were not always taken at face value, as one 40-year-old widow and mother of six found. In January 1677, the woman claimed to have miscarried when her lodger saw evidence that she had given birth recently, presumably bloodied and stained linen. However the lodger, who appeared as witness for the prosecution, had reportedly found a 'perfect' baby hidden in a box on a shelf, with signs of scissor wounds on its head. The woman's claim of insanity was thrown out and the death sentence imposed, because of the careful concealment of the body.

One factor which could have swayed the jury in the first case is that the woman was married to a man of good reputation, and that the baby was well provided for. In cases where the woman had concealed her pregnancy and had not prepared a layette ready for the birth, then the charge of infanticide was much more likely to result in a guilty verdict. An example of this can be seen in the trial of Mary Bucknal in September 1680. Mary gave birth in the bedroom she shared with another woman, but tried desperately to hide her labour from her companion.

When her bedfellow awoke and asked what was the matter, she passed off her grunts and groans by claiming that 'she had bought the day before one penny worth of damsons, and that by eating them she had surfeited herself, the which had caused her to vomit,' which the woman accepted, given that excessive consumption of fruit was well-known to be bad for you, and went back to sleep. Mary hid the body of her newborn son between the base of the bed and the mattress and when it was discovered, she claimed the baby had been stillborn. She was committed to be hanged for murder, since she had kept the pregnancy hidden and did not appear to have made any provision for caring for the baby after the birth.

In one infamous infanticide case from 1650, 22-year-old Anne Greene was convicted of having murdered her baby. She had conceived the child during an affair with a member of Sir Thomas Reed's household, in which she worked as a servant. Anne was accused of having 'overworked' herself 'turning malt' and, in so doing, deliberately caused a miscarriage when she was about four months pregnant. She delivered the foetus, which was too small for its sex to be determined, on the toilet 'the jakes,' and it was found hidden in the corner of the privy, after a search by suspicious fellow workers who saw the blood stains on her clothes and bed-linen. The baby was covered in the ashes and dust usually thrown down the toilet to prevent foul odours. Anne maintained throughout that she had not known she was pregnant, as she had still been having her periods, and she had gone to the toilet with stomach cramps and no idea that she had miscarried.

As a single woman, under a 1624 law to 'Prevent the Destroying and Murdering of Bastard Children' Anne was automatically presumed guilty, because she concealed the birth, and so she was hanged in the courtyard of Oxford Castle. Executions happened in public until The Capital Punishment Amendment Act of 1868. Often a large crowd gathered to watch. Gaols often had portable gallows, which could be erected near the site of a crime as some courts ordered convicts to be hanged near the place their crime occurred.

Convicts were driven to their deaths in an open cart, with their hands tied behind their backs, as public humiliation was considered to be an integral aspect of the punishment. In Anne's case, it took her over half an hour to die and several friends had to pull her legs down to help her suffocate more quickly. Anne was eventually declared dead and her body taken to the office of Thomas Willis, a famous Oxford physician, who wished to dissect her. Courts often granted medics the right to a number of convicts' bodies per year, as they were the only corpses legally allowed to be used for dissection.

However, back at Willis' house some rattling in Anne's throat was heard and she was revived. The doctors let her blood and put her in a warm bed. By the next day Anne had revived sufficiently to speak, much to everyone's amazement. There was a general feeling that this was a sign of divine intervention, and that Anne must therefore be innocent. As the subject of a miracle, Anne was visited by thousands of curious strangers. After her miraculous recovery gained her a pardon, she went on to marry, have children and lived a normal life in the country.

Bigamy

In the 1660s a woman from Canterbury, who had been born Mary Stedman but was also known by the aliases Maria de Wolway and Mary Moders, but most usually as Mary Carleton, and even 'the German Princess,' became something of a celebrity in 1663, during her trial for bigamy. She seems to have revelled in her notoriety throughout the next decade. The case presented to the court was that Mary had married John Carleton bigamously, being already married to a cobbler from her home town of Canterbury.

In the run-up to the trial various pamphlets appeared, claiming that Mary was a well-known thief and con-artist, but the judge dismissed this as hearsay. The main charge against her was that she had passed herself off as a German princess who had vast wealth. Her money had attracted Carleton, a lawyer's clerk whose sister ran the pub in which Mary lodged. Mary was acquitted because, although a witness to her first marriage was found to give evidence, her first husband did not appear and so the judge accepted her defence that she believed him to be dead. Sometime between leaving the cobbler and reappearing in London, Mary had acquired some rich clothing, which enabled her to pass herself off as a noblewoman.

Following the trial, Mary responded to the pamphlets against her in *The Case of Madam Mary Carleton*. Here, she admitted to pretending to be a princess, but declared 'what harm have I done in pretending to great titles?' The main reason she was imprisoned and brought to trial, she claimed, was that the Carletons wanted to be rid of her once they discovered that she was not wealthy. However, she counter-claimed that she had been tricked into the marriage, as John Carleton told her that he was himself a lord and the son of an earl. A play written by Thomas Parker about this story, in which Mary herself took the lead role, was staged – although it only ran for one night.

In real life, Mary's story did not have a happy ending and, after her brief time in the spotlight, she was again arrested in 1671 and sentenced to be transported to Jamaica. Somehow she managed to get back to England, in contravention of her deportation order, and was arrested for theft again in 1673. Because of her fame, she was recognised as the notorious 'German princess' by a gaoler, and since she had previously been transported for theft, this time she was hanged at Tyburn.

The title of 'German Princess' was seized upon by publisher George Croom to sell copies of an account of the activities of criminal Jenny Voss. Voss was a repeat offender like Carleton, and similarly had been transported, only to return illicitly to England. According to the pamphlet, she was notorious across Europe. After she was hanged at Tyburn in December 1684, Croom published what he claimed was an 'account of the life and death of Jenney Voss [...] published from her own confession.' Significantly though, he called the pamphlet *The German Princess Revived; or The London Jilt*. The latter title is taken from a salacious fictional autobiography of a London prostitute published the same year. Both titles suggest that Croom was aiming at the market for sensational texts. The official court transcripts were themselves published from the Old Bailey eight times a year from 1674, and sold in vast numbers.

Burglary and Murder

Mary Carleton's fame was due, in part, to the spirited way in which she conducted her own defence. Indeed, Mary herself reminded the jury during her 1663 trial, 'if guilty, she must die; a woman has no clergy' in serious cases, and while this argument might have swayed the jury in her original trial, there was no choice at her subsequent theft trial because she was a repeat offender and had returned despite being transported, leaving execution as the only option for the court.

Burglary and murder were crimes for which the benefit could not be invoked, but in the early eighteenth century defendant Sarah Malcolm

(1710–1733) was just as outspoken in her own defence as Mary Carleton had been. On 4 February 1733 Sarah murdered three women. She stabbed Ann Price in the throat and strangled Lydia Duncomb an 80-year-old widow, along with her elderly maid, Elizabeth Harrison. She was also indicted for stealing 20 moidores (Portuguese gold coins), 18 guineas, and various other items, including a silver tankard and two smocks. Sarah pleaded not guilty to all the charges.

What is remarkable about Sarah's defence is that, when questioned about her bloodied clothing, she claimed:

Modesty might compel a Woman to conceal her own Secrets if Necessity did not oblige her to the contrary; and 'tis Necessity that obliges me to say, that what has been taken for the Blood of the murdered Person is nothing but the free Gift of Nature. This was all that appeared on my Shift, and it was the same on my Apron, for I wore the Apron under me next to my Shift.

In an age when women never publicly discussed their menstrual cycles, Sarah claimed in open court that the blood on her clothes was due to her period, not that of the woman she had stabbed. Sarah probably had been menstruating at this time, because when she was subjected to a physical examination in prison, Roger Johnson, her gaoler, who claimed to have had orders to search her, said that Sarah asked him not to examine her, 'because she was not in a condition.' To prove that she was menstruating, Sarah showed Johnson her shift, 'upon which I desisted.' However, the jury was unimpressed with these claims and Sarah was found guilty on all counts.

Like Mary Carleton, Sarah attracted notoriety and her priest published a book purportedly containing Sarah's confession, *A True Copy of the Paper, Delivered the Night Before her Execution, by Sarah Malcom [sic.] to the Rev. Mr. Piddington*, which he claimed had been sent to him by Sarah herself. She even had two drawings made of her by the famous eighteenth century artist William Hogarth.

Hoaxers and Confidence Tricksters

Not all notorious crimes were as gruesome as Malcolm's, however, but many people did commit frauds which would be impossible to pass off today. In 1726 a woman from Godalming in Surrey became famous for claiming that she had given birth to a number of rabbits. In August Mary Toft (1703–1763) suffered a miscarriage after seeing a rabbit. A common belief at the time was that rabbits could signify trouble in pregnancy, and some writers claimed that the mother catching sight of a rabbit could result in a baby being born with a cleft, or as it was then known 'hare' lip.

The miscarriage story would then not have seemed implausible to an eighteenth century audience. The difference in Mary Toft's case was that she claimed the miscarriage had not produced a baby, but parts of a monstrous birth resembling a rabbit. The story was backed up by her midwife mother-in-law Ann, who a month afterwards cut up a cat, a rabbit and an eel and took these animal body parts for the local man-midwife, John Howard, to examine pretending they were part of the matter produced by the miscarriage.

The pair seem to have drawn Howard into the scam and he moved Mary to his home in Guildford, where she was apparently giving birth to a rabbit most days. Mary was displayed to audiences including both nobility and ordinary townspeople, who claimed to be able to make out the rabbits jumping in her swollen abdomen. Nathanael St Andre, surgeon and anatomist to the royal household, and Samuel Molyneux, private secretary to the Prince of Wales, went to Howard's house and claimed to have witnessed the birth of the fifteenth rabbit. The story eventually caught the King's ear and Mary was ordered to London. Like that of Sarah Malcolm, the Toft case inspired a drawing by William Hogarth, who depicted the birthing room and many of Mary's famous attendants.

The fraud continued until December that year, when Mary's sister-in-law was found to have been buying rabbits for use in the stunt. Their method had been to insert animal parts into Mary's womb, while the cervix was still pliable following her miscarriage. She could then deliver rabbits on demand. Mary was sent to Tothill Fields Prison at Bridewell, and the following month she and Howard appeared in court, where he was fined £800 for his involvement in the scam.

This sum was a substantial amount, no doubt deliberately punitive given the establishment figures that Howard had embarrassed, and which might equate to several years' income, even for a professional man. According to *The Proceedings of the Old Bailey*, at this time a domestic servant would earn £2–3 a year, and an income of £40 was needed to comfortably keep a family. A middling sort of family would need a minimum of £100 a year to keep a small household with, whereas someone with an income of £500 was considered wealthy.

Mary was released from prison in April, when the case against her was quietly dropped, and she returned to Godalming, where she lived out the rest of her days until 1763. Her case and those described above, show women committing often very serious crimes. What most of these stories have in common is the direct relationship between the crime and women's statuses as maids, wives, and mothers. Infanticide was seen as the only way to get out of an unbearable situation by some reluctant mothers, as petty-treason was by some wives.

Women's bodies were also at the centre of their crimes. Sarah Malcolm's murder trial hinged on the question of whether the blood found on her was from her reproductive body, or the murdered women, and Mary Toft exploited her reproductive organs for fame and fortune.

Chapter Fourteen

Women and Politics

The time period covered by this book is framed just beyond the reigns of two women, Elizabeth I and Anne I, yet early modern society operated on a strict patriarchal hierarchy. Common stereotypes dictated that women might be silent in public, but were often nagging scolds behind closed doors. Discussing the nature of marriage in his book on women's rights, the lawyer Thomas Edgar wrote in 1632 that, although a married couple became one person in law, it was necessary to understand the way this dynamic worked from the woman's perspective:

> *wedlock is a locking together. It is true, that man and wife are one person; but understand in what manner. When a small brook or a little rivulet incorporates with Rhodanus* [the Rhone], *Humber, or Thames, the poor rivulet loses her name; it is carried and recarried with the new associate; it bears no sway.*

On marriage woman lost her individual legal status, becoming a *femme covert* she was now envisaged as a stream subsumed into a wide river. The law, the Church, and medical authorities all agreed that, while men and women had been designed to fit together and work as a couple, each with their distinct qualities and roles, this partnership was on the understanding that men were the leaders made in the image of God, while women were made to be helpmates, from his flesh.

In pre-Christian times Aristotle had claimed that women were 'deformed men,' conceived when the conditions in the womb were less than perfect. This idea was reproduced in some early modern medical books. Women were also thought less capable of rational thought than men, and there was even a debate about whether women possessed immortal souls. The famous poet and preacher John Donne debated this in some of his early writings, which were only published after his death.

Of course, not everyone held with the view that women were less human than men, and in 1658, for example, William Austin wrote, in the *Excellency of the Creation of Women*, that men and women differed

> *only in the body. For, she has the same reasonable soul; and, in that, there is neither hes, nor shes; neither excellency, nor superiority: she hath the same soul, the same mind; the same understanding; and tends to the same end of eternal salvation that he does.*

Underpinning the legal and cultural prejudice against women was the biblical story of Eve. Her transgression in taking the fruit from the Tree of Knowledge had caused the Fall of Man and expulsion from the Garden of Eden. Because of her action, men had to work for their living, women suffered pain in childbirth and menstruation and had to be ruled by their husbands. The fact that all women were considered to be descendants of Eve led to assumptions that, like their ancestress, women were necessarily more highly-sexed and less cerebral than men.

As a result of their innate sinful nature, it was believed that women had to be ruled like children. The early modern social hierarchy placed God as the head of all, followed by his representative on earth, the monarch, who, as James I always stressed, was like a father to his nation, and this pattern was mirrored on a domestic level by the father or husband presiding over the other inhabitants within a household. This social order reveals why the killing of a husband was classed in law as petty-treason, rather than murder.

To prevent the fact of her gender from disrupting this hierarchy, when she was queen, Elizabeth I described herself in her official, public capacity as a Prince, even through she was a woman. Famously a history of England by Samuel Clarke, *England's Remembrancer*, in 1677 describes how, in the so-called Tilbury speech, which she is reputed to have given on the eve of the Spanish invasion, Elizabeth I is recorded as saying: 'I know I have the body but of a weak and feeble Woman, but I have the Heart and Stomach of a King, and of a King of England too.'

What did Early Modern Women Think of Eve's Sin?

Women seem to have broadly accepted their lower legal status and conformed to their husbands and fathers' wishes, in the main. That is not to suggest that they were passive and voiceless, but rather that this order, considered to have been ordained by God, was accepted as the way things were by most people.

For this reason even the most vocal defences of women were written within these parameters. In the ground-breaking poem, 'Salve Deus Rex Judaeorum' by Amelia Lanyer (1569–1645), published in 1611, Lanyer defends Eve using the argument that she may have been tricked by the cunning serpent, but Adam had committed a greater transgression in eating the fruit, since he should have known better:

> *If Eve did err, it was for knowledge sake,*
> *The fruit being faire persuaded him to fall:*
> *No subtle Serpent's falsehood did betray him,*
> *If he would eat it, who had power to stay* [stop] *him?*

Eve's true fault, Amelia argued, was to love Adam too much, which made her want to share the fruit she had been tricked into tasting with him. The poet firmly placed all the responsibility upon Adam:

> *If any evil did in her remain,*
> *Being made of him, he was the ground of all [...]*
> *Her weakness did the serpent's words obey,*
> *But you in malice Gods dear Son betray.*

Amelia Lanyer was the daughter of a court musician, and she had been educated beyond the norms for a girl of her standing, in the service of both the Dowager Countess of Kent and of the household the Countess of Cumberland. She was in no doubt that women should be seen as being at the heart of Christian theology, complaining that men should not forget that 'it pleased our Lord and Saviour Jesus Christ, without the assistance of man [...] to be begotten of a woman, borne of a woman, obedient to a woman' and that in his lifetime he had 'healed woman, pardoned women, comforted women.' She even pointed out that Jesus 'after his resurrection, appeared first to a woman, sent a woman to declare his most glorious resurrection to the rest of his Disciples,' which, she says, should mean that 'honourable minded men' should 'speak reverently of our sex, and especially of all virtuous and good women.'

The position of women as an inferior version of the male, and one who would be inevitably tainted by the sin of Eve, was being questioned as early as 1589, when Jane Anger (possibly a pseudonym, as the author admits to writing in a 'choleric vein,' in which 'Anger shall reap anger') wrote a spirited defence of her sex, claiming:

The creation of man and woman at the first, he being formed in principio *of dross and filthy clay, did so remain until God saw that in him his workmanship was good, and therefore by the transformation of the dust which was loathsome unto flesh, it became purified. Then lacking a help for him, God making woman of man's flesh, that she might be purer than he, does evidently show, how far we women are more excellent than men.*

The reason for female superiority, the author wrote, was because women could give birth: 'Our bodies are fruitful, whereby the world increases, our care wonderful, by which man is preserved.' Just like Amelia Lanyer, Jane Anger argued that, 'From woman sprang man's salvation. A woman was the first that believed, and a woman likewise the first that repented of sin.'

The writer Ester Sowernam (potentially the pseudonym of a Joan Sharp) also published on this topic. Sowernam's pamphlet *Ester Hath Hang'd Haman* (1617) was a direct response to Joseph Swetnam's *Arraignment of Women* (1615), a deeply misogynistic text. Addressed to the female reader, Sowernam's text is split into four sections, with the first using scripture to prove the 'dignity and worthiness' of women. The pamphlet makes deliberately provocative claims, for instance that Eve was created to perfect God's prototype in Adam, and that the serpent who brought about man's downfall was male, which vindicates Eve, who played the part of duped victim in the tragedy, culpable 'but not in so high a degree as the man.' The second section uses non-religious texts to emphasise the bravery of women, from Helen of Troy to Elizabeth I.

Sowernam points out the double standard in society whereby women were at the mercy of their reputations, but men experienced no such repercussions for moral or sexual indiscretions. The third section is a direct response to Swetnam, which refuted his claim that women were responsible for sin by pointing out that Adam was meant to lead his wife, again making him, rather than Eve, culpable.

Significantly, Ester described herself as 'neither maid, wife nor widow, yet really all, and therefore experienced to defend all,' a status that she felt gave her the authority to speak out for all women. Ester's rejection of the conventional triad of womanly roles can be seen as a reaction to, and rejection of, the way in which Swetnam used it to abuse women in his book. This might also explain her choice of pseudonym, with 'sour' being the opposite of his 'sweet.' Ester's text was one of at least eight rebuttals, by or purported to be by, women published in response to Joseph Swetnam.

The most famous response to Swetnam and the only one that was not published under a pen name and so was definitely by a woman was by Rachel Speght (c1597–c1661), the daughter of a Calvinist minister. Her pamphlet defending women, *A Mouzell for Melastomus* (1617), recognises that Swetnam was being deliberately controversial, calling him a 'baiter of women.' She argued that fear of God should have made Swetnam hold back, but that Satan had obviously got inside his quill. She made the case that 'man was as an imperfect building afore woman was made; and bringing her unto Adam, united and married them together,' to show that each sex was uniquely valued before God as necessary for mankind's future.

In this Rachel Speght wasn't challenging the assumed natural order of man as head of the family but instead arguing that each half of a married couple was expected to offer their individual qualities in marriage. Rachel herself married a minister and did not publish any more pamphlets in later life.

Women in the Civil Wars

Religious and political tensions between King Charles I and Parliament culminated in a series of civil wars in England between 1642 and 1651. In 1643 the failure of Parliament to reach a compromise with the king caused anger and frustration among the women of London. Women of the city had been surprisingly vocal and, in a letter to his wife dated 9 August that year, Sir

Thomas Knyvett reported how a 'multitude' of up to 300 women gathered outside parliament to protest for peace. The women all wore white ribbons in their hats, showing that this was an organised, rather than spontaneous protest. Apparently unconvinced by the reassurances they were offered, they returned the next day with their numbers swollen to around 5,000.

The ability the ensuing Civil Wars would have to divide the population is evidenced in one story from this second day of protest. A spectacle maker from Westminster Hall, John Norman, was ranting about the futility of the women's protest, which had by now turned violent, when he was told one of the women had been shot dead. According to Knyvett, Norman responded that it was 'no matter if a hundred of them were served so.'

However, after going to join the crowds to see what had happened, Norman discovered the woman who had been killed was in fact his own daughter, an apprentice seamstress, who had been sent on an errand unconnected with the protest. The soldier who shot her was investigated, but he claimed that his pistol had fired by mischance rather than intentionally. The women were disparaged in contemporary writings as oyster wenches, which was a slang term used for lower class women, commentators using the term to suggest that only low ranking women would act in such an indecorous way.

The Civil Wars saw women of all ranks of society become involved in politics, however. Lady Anne Halkett described in her autobiography how she was involved with the 14-year-old Duke of York, later King James II's flight to France. The Duke was in the custody of the Earl of Northumberland, and Anne was at that time involved in an illicit relationship with a soldier, Colonel Joseph Bampfield, a royalist supporter. Bampfield gained permission to visit James, and Anne asked him to take a ribbon with him to secretly measure the young man's waist and height, so that she could order a woman's dress for him as a disguise. Anne's tailor queried the measurements, saying that although he had made hundreds of dresses, he had never been asked to make one for a woman as short as this with so large a waist, but, of course, the measurements were for a teenage boy.

The escape plan was remarkably simple. In the run up to the escape the Duke established a habit of playing hide and seek with his younger siblings in the garden after supper each night, so that on the day of his escape people would assume he was merely 'at his usual sport.' Bampfield waited at the garden gate with a periwig and a cloak, before taking the Duke down river to a safe house, where Anne and her maid Miriam were waiting with the costume. Anne was in a state of high tension because Bampfield had warned her to flee if the party didn't arrive by 10pm, as that would mean they had been discovered and she might be incriminated.

However, although they took longer than anticipated, Anne was resolved to see through her promise to help the Duke. His boat had to row against the wind and the party was almost caught out boarding a ship at Gravesend but for another woman, Colonel Washington's wife who stepped in to cover for them, and he made a successful escape to the Netherlands.

On the other side of the political divide, Brilliana, Lady Harley, the third wife of Sir Robert Harley, was left to defend the Harley castle at Brampton Bryan, near the Welsh borders. Sir Robert, a Parliamentarian, was mainly in London during the wars and his wife was left quite isolated, living in a Royalist area. In December 1642, she was notified by the Governor of Hereford that she should hand over her castle to the King and, on her refusal, a siege began the following July. She put up a spirited resistance and, when it became clear during an agreed ceasefire that the Royalist troops were moving their gun carriages, she ordered her troops to shoot at them, killing a number of men.

Eventually Parliamentarian Lord Fairfax's army reached Gloucester and the Royalists were redeployed and the siege ended. They did not stay away long, and within months were threatening the castle again. During the siege, fearful of the danger she was in, Brilliana regularly wrote to her husband telling him how she worried for her and her children's lives and asking for his permission to leave the castle, but this was not forthcoming. The effects of this stress cost Brilliana her health and she died of 'apoplexy and defluxion of the lungs' in October 1643. Without her leadership, the castle fell in early 1644.

There are many accounts of women petitioning for their husband's cause at this time. Margaret Cavendish, Duchess of Newcastle, returned from the continent, where she had lived at the exiled Charles II's court with her husband the Duke of Newcastle, to plead for some of the money which had been confiscated or sequestered when the Duke had fled the country. Men would face arrest if they returned home, and so it was left to their wives to fight their cause on their behalf.

Sir Ralph Verney was also in exile, despite being on the opposite side politically to most of the exiled Royalists. Verney was anti-William Laud, the Archbishop of London, and disapproved of his reforms to the Anglican Church, and was a member of parliament on the Parliamentary side. Due to his religious principles, he felt unable to sign the Solemn League and Covenant in 1643 (an agreement between the English Parliament and Scotland to fight against the Irish Catholics, in return for England adopting some aspects of Scottish governance), so he felt obliged to flee too.

The Verneys were a family divided by the Civil Wars, and life in exile had left the family short of money, so his wife Lady Mary returned to England to sue for the return of their property. It took a few attempts but Mary was eventually successful in her plea, arguing that Ralph was only guilty of absence, not of being against Parliament. However, upon her return to Blois to be reunited with her husband and children, Mary died aged 34. Ralph never remarried during his remaining 46 years.

In November 1642, Leveller and later Quaker activist John Lilburne was the first Roundhead (Parliamentarian) soldier to be captured by the Royalists and imprisoned at Oxford Castle. His wife Elizabeth went to Parliament to petition on his behalf continuously, despite the fact that she was pregnant. Lilburne and his fellow prisoners were due to be executed for treason on 20 December, but as a result of Elizabeth's actions, Parliament published a notice on 18 December that if the execution went ahead then they would retaliate by executing Royalist prisoners. Elizabeth herself took the news to Lilburne's captors in Oxford. The trial was called off and in May 1643, Lilburne was exchanged for a high profile Royalist. Elizabeth Lilburne went to great lengths to fight for her husband's political cause, as did Mary Overton, the wife of fellow Leveller Richard Overton, the publisher of Lilburne's political pamphlets. Overton was imprisoned in 1646 and Mary, along with her brother, continued his work.

In January 1647 Mary was arrested, after being found producing an illegal anti-Royalist pamphlet, *Regal Tyranny*. Mary, pregnant again despite having given birth in the previous August, refused to say who brought the manuscript to her shop, then refused her arrest and reports say she was dragged, with her infant in her arms through the streets to Bridewell, with the arresting officers calling her a wild whore and a strumpet. Mary sent petitions to parliament for her release, without success, and her baby was born and died in prison, before her eventual release, the following July.

One elite woman, Elizabeth Murray, Duchess of Dysart (1626–1698) was highly unusual in that, as the eldest of her father's five daughters, she inherited his dukedom in her own right. Elizabeth was highly intelligent and educated; she outwardly appeared to conform to the conventions of a noble wife and had 11 children in quick succession, following her marriage in 1648. However, at her home in Richmond she feigned a friendship with Oliver Cromwell, which was in fact a cover for her activities in support of the Royalist cause. In 1653 the Duchess joined the Sealed Knot, a secret society working to secure the Restoration of Charles II. Elizabeth was so convincing that she was able to travel abroad on spying trips and even meet up with the King, all without attracting suspicion. On the King's Restoration, Elizabeth was rewarded with a pension of £800 a year.

Women and Politics in the Late Seventeenth-Century

The pattern of women petitioning for their husbands continued after the Restoration too. John Bunyan wrote about how when he was in prison for repeatedly breaching the peace by preaching, his wife Elizabeth went to appeal to the courts for his release. Bunyan had been hoping to get a pardon as part of the King's coronation celebrations in April 1661, but he wasn't successful.

Elizabeth went three times to judges to argue his case; she pleaded that she needed her husband at home to support their four children (her step-children, from Bunyan's previous marriage), one of whom was blind. To emphasise the strain her husband's imprisonment was having on her, Elizabeth revealed that she had been pregnant when he was first arrested in January, but the shock of this had caused her to miscarry, after a painful eight-day labour. Bunyan was kept in prison because he refused to promise to stop preaching; he did not gain his freedom until 1672.

After the turmoil of the Civil Wars and the Restoration period, women spoke out about their position in society more and began to challenge the idea that they were not entitled to the same educational opportunities as men and dispute the belief that they should be submissive in marriage too.

In 1673, Bathsua Makin (1600–c.1675), a renowned scholar, and tutor to the Stuart Princesses published *An Essay to Revive the Ancient Education of Gentlewomen*. Dedicated to Princess (later Queen) Mary, the daughter of James II, the book is undoubtedly political, as it suggests that men would not easily accept a change to the *status quo* when it already gave them all the advantages of education.

While giving examples of women who have benefited from a high level education, Bathsua lists 'The Princess Elizabeth, daughter to King Charles the first, to whom Mrs. Makin was tutoress, [*who*] at nine years old could write, read, and in some measure understand, Latin, Greek, Hebrew, French and Italian.' She included classical scholars, such as Hypatia (350–415), the Alexandrian scholar, whose mathematical theories are still used today, and who was later martyred, and Sappho the Greek poet. Of her contemporaries, Bathsua cites the poets Anne Bradstreet and Katherine Philips.

The context of Bathsua's radical arguments, though, remained firmly rooted within the social hierarchy of the times: she did not advocate more than a basic education for lower class women, only gentlewomen; she is similarly scathing about women belonging to other cultures and religions. She also acknowledged a need for gentlewomen to be grounded in traditional feminine skills, like sewing:

I do not deny but women ought to be brought up to a comely and decent carriage, to their needle, to neatness, to understand all those things that do particularly belong to their sex. But when these things are competently cared for, and where there are endowments of nature and leisure, then higher things ought to be endeavoured after. Merely to teach gentlewomen to frisk and dance, to paint their faces, to curl their hair, to put on a whisk, to wear gay clothes, is not truly to adorn, but to adulterate their bodies; yea, (what is worse) to defile their souls.

Mary Astell (1666–1731) took on and developed this argument in her book, *A Serious Proposal to the Ladies* (1694). She argued that women were often silly and preoccupied with trivial things, but this was simply because of their lack of education. This deficiency, she claimed, led them into the temptation to sin because they knew no better; essentially, she was arguing that it was a parent's moral obligation to educate their daughters to be able to make informed life choices.

Mary was part of a circle of educated upper-class women, along with Judith Drake, Mary Chudleigh and several others. Judith Drake was the wife of the physician James Drake and she often worked alongside him in his medical practice; when her husband died in 1707 she edited and published his best-known work, the anatomy guide *Anthropologia Nova*. She published her own book, *An Essay in Defence of the Female Sex* (1696), anonymously, as Mary Astell had done, but this led people to assume for many years that Astell had written it. In this book Judith argued that men and women were intellectually equal but, out of fear of women's capabilities, men had limited their access to education over the ages.

The radicalism advocated by Mary Chudleigh (1656–1710) developed this and in her poem 'To the Ladies,' she argued that 'Wife and servant are the same, / But only differ in the name.' Chudleigh published *The Ladies Defence; Or, a Dialogue Between Sir John Brute, Sir William Loveall, Melissa, and a Parson*, in 1701, after being urged to publish it by friends who had read it in manuscript form. *The Ladies' Defence* was, like the works of Ester Sowernam and Rachel Speght, written in response to a publication by a man, in this case a wedding sermon, *The Bride-Woman's Counsellor*, published by John Sprint the year before. This work described how the true role of all women was to love, honour, and be obedient to their husbands.

Mary's poem, 'To the Ladies,' retorted that, if a woman's role on marriage was to be mute and subservient, then they should 'then shun, oh! shun that wretched state.' This kind of radicalism faded after the early eighteenth century and, although there were notable women advocating female rights throughout this time, women's lives became more restricted to the domestic sphere as that century progressed.

Chapter Fifteen

Literary Women

It has been estimated that by the mid-seventeenth century no more than 10 per cent of women in England could sign their name. Literacy rates were then much higher among men than women and clustered heavily in the cities and towns. Reading and writing were taught as separate subjects at schools, which were mostly attended by boys, and within the home. Acquiring one skill did not necessarily lead to the other, which may indicate that more women were able to read than these figures suggest.

Historians usually judge literacy by whether or not someone could sign their name, but acknowledge that this does not always accurately reflect the situation. For instance, in October 1699 apothecary John Westover asked his sister, Hannah Poole, and Ann Wall, his 'washerwoman,' to witness a legal document for him. It is impossible from this record to deduce whether either woman could write much beyond making their signature. The low level of literacy among the population, and particularly among women, obviously affects how representative surviving early modern writings are of the issues and topics that mattered to women, especially those outside the elite, at the time. The number of extant spiritual diaries by upper-class women might offer a sense that women in general were more pious than they really were, for example.

The amount of writing by women from this period which survives today is, however, astonishingly varied. Texts range from diaries, letters, commonplace books, recipe books, poetry, plays, romance fiction, instructional texts, conversion narratives, autobiographies and biographies, translations, travel writings and many more. Commonplace books have been compared to the ubiquitous Filofaxes of the last century, essentially places to jot down any recipes, events, contacts, pieces of doctrine that you enjoyed at church or anecdotes you wanted to keep. Maintaining a commonplace book was encouraged by the reformed religion as part of personal reflection on your piety, and both men and women made use of them. Just because they were not printed or formally published did not mean that this form of writing was not made public.

Manuscript circulation was a form of publication among upper-class intellectual circles which flourished at this time. For instance, in the early seventeenth century Lady Dionys Fitzherbert had the account she had written detailing her religious crisis copied out twice by scribes, then sent out to different readers. In her three-volume autobiography, Alice Thornton covered the years from her birth in February 1627 to the time of writing, 1669.

In it, Alice claimed she was writing the text to vindicate her good name, after her late sister's daughter, Anne Danby, and a former servant, Mary Breaks, had spread rumours that she had had a sexual liaison with a Thomas Comber, when she was then in marriage negotiations on behalf of her young daughter. Comber was the family chaplain at the Thorntons' home, East Newton Hall, and both Alice and her husband were fond of him, and so approved his betrothal to their daughter Alice, who was then only 12, especially since he had offered to wait a number of years until Alice was older, to marry her. The daughter and the chaplain did, in fact, marry in secret on 17 November 1668, when Alice was 14.

Many of these personal forms of writing remained unpublished during the author's lifetime but appeared in print posthumously in some instances, such as when the poems of Katherine Philips (1632–1664) appeared in 1667 as *Poems by the Most Deservedly Admired Mrs Katherine Philips, the Matchless Orinda* (an unauthorised edition of her poetry had been published in the year of her death, 1664, published without her knowledge or consent). The act of writing for publication pushed the boundaries of acceptable female behaviour in the seventeenth century.

Margaret Cavendish, Duchess of Newcastle, broke convention to publish openly in her own name. Margaret was well aware of the censure that her decision to publish would bring and faced it head-on in the address to the female reader of her first work, *Poems and Fancies* (1653), saying 'condemn not as a dishonour of your sex, for setting forth this work; for it is harmless and free from all dishonesty.' Publishing drew attention to women in ways which went against the codes of expected behaviour at this time when they were meant to be submissive in public at least.

Other texts, like Alice Thornton's, were published in the nineteenth century, when there was a fashion for discovering and printing early modern manuscript writings. Among the works printed at this time were Elizabeth, Viscountess of Mordaunt's private diaries, and the letters of Brilliana, Lady Harley. While the Victorians did much to preserve seventeenth century diaries, the nineteenth century editors regularly left out the parts pertaining to anything 'improper' and so women's accounts of sexual relationships and childbirths were often removed.

Some women wrote neither for praise nor for posterity. The poems of Gertrude Thimelby show that she wrote some of them as thrifty presents. Gertrude discussed being impoverished in some verses and claimed that the poem she wrote to her sister-in-law, 'To the Lady Elizabeth Thimelby on New Year's Day 1655,' was in place of the traditional New Year gift that higher-ranking people exchanged. The travel memoirs of Celia Fiennes were also written for her own pleasure, and published in the nineteenth century.

Between 1684 and the early eighteenth century, Celia travelled throughout England on horseback, sometimes only accompanied by a servant, and constantly documenting her visits and experiences. A book based on her memoirs first appeared in 1888, entitled *Through England on a Side Saddle in the Time of William and Mary*. This was true too of Lucy Hutchinson's (1620–1681) biography of her husband, *A Memoir of the Life of Colonel Hutchinson*, which was first published in 1806. Lucy was a serious scholar who made translations of Latin works and described in her autobiography, which was published with her husband's biography, her disdain for the traditional female pursuits: 'As for music and dancing, I profited very little in them, and would never practise my lute or harpsichord but when my masters were with me; and for my needle I absolutely hated it.'

This chapter concentrates on the published works of women in early modern England and the circumstances in which these texts were produced to give a flavour of the variety of women's writing that got into print. One consequence of the Civil Wars was the temporary end of licensing for books, which facilitated a print explosion that occurred into the 1650s. This tidal wave of new works included many publications by women, several of which will be discussed below.

Advisory Texts and Religious Works

Older women passing on advice to younger ones was considered a particularly acceptable format for women's writing, and several authors, such as Anne Murray, Lady Halkett (whose 'Meditations, Prayers, and a Mother's Legacy' still exists in manuscript form) used this genre. A number of women published accounts of their spiritual conversion, meant to serve both as proof of their own piety but also as an example for younger women to follow.

Several short pamphlets known as mothers' legacies appeared in print too. These include those of Dorothy Leigh (1616), Elizabeth Joscelin (1622) and Elizabeth Richardson (1645), and the authors wrote as mothers giving instructions to their children in the event of their deaths. These women were both reflecting a genuine fear of death in childbirth but also practising an acceptable literary form for women. Dorothy Leigh's book was addressed to her sons and entitled *The Mother's Blessing, or the Godly Counsel of a Gentlewoman Not Long Since Deceased, Left Behind for Her Children*. It went on to be republished in over 20 editions. Her fellow 'mother's legacy' author, Elizabeth Joscelin wrote that it would be strange for a child to read the words of a mother who had died in childbirth, which was prophetic as she died in 1622 nine days after her daughter's birth.

Dorothy Leigh's advice to her infant sons was extremely detailed and even included how they should behave on marriage, tips on rearing their own children and what sort of names she would like her grandchildren to be called. By contrast Elizabeth Richardson, Baroness Cramond's motherly advice and prayer book *A Ladies Legacy to her Daughters* was addressed solely to her four daughters and excluded her two sons. Elizabeth reworked her original 1625 text for the presses some years later.

More esoteric forms of advice could be found in almanacs, pamphlets filled with astrological charts and predictions for the year ahead, which were hugely popular in the period. Sarah Jinner produced several between 1658 and 1664, and her success led a satirist to create a spin-off 1659 almanac specifically aimed at women. This edition was not by Jinner herself, as the author is given as 'Sarah Ginnor' and the text is a deeply misogynistic parody, but does show that her almanacs had made an impact if they were thought worth cashing in on.

Jinner's almanacs contained advice on topics such as medical cures for pregnant women and menstrual problems, as well as all the usual astrological predictions for the year ahead. In the 1659 edition, for example, Jinner gives recipes to 'provoke the terms' or bring on a period; three to stop heavy bleeding. Her oil to bring down periods consists of oil of almonds, an ounce of white lilies mixed with oil of aniseed, and made into an ointment.

In 1688 and 1689, another woman, Mary Holden, also published almanacs. She described herself as both a midwife and a student of astronomy, and her almanac contains practical advice, for example that peas should be sown in January and that you should put your mares 'to horse' in May to conceive foals. It also contains conversion tables to work out everything from when Easter will next fall and the value of the pound. Almanacs sold in vast quantities and were consulted by men and women; as contemporary jokes suggested, at the end of the year they provided another service, when their readers recycled them as toilet paper.

Medical Texts and Receipt Books

Many women wrote recipe (receipt) books full of medical preparations, and so we might expect to find a range of printed medical advice books by early modern women, yet they are few and far between. In 1653, a book purportedly based on Elizabeth, the Countess of Kent's receipt book was published and it went on to be reprinted for several decades. *A Choice Manual of Rare and Select Secrets in Physick and Surgery*, offered recipes to cure all manner of illnesses – from dry coughs, to childbirth pains, and even the plague. Some of these cures now seem quite unappealing, such as the instruction to cure a bleeding wound by taking a 'hound's turd' and placing it on a hot coal, before applying it to a wound to staunch it.

It wasn't until 1671 that the first English midwifery guide by a woman was published. Experienced midwife Jane Sharp's *The Midwives Book* was marketed as a guide for her sister midwives. The book takes its medical knowledge from established male authors, such as Daniel Sennert and Nicholas Culpeper, but crucially Sharp modified some of the men's strictures at times when her own beliefs, based on her years of practice, ran contrary to received wisdom. The book carried a defence of female birth attendants, reminding readers that there is no mention of men-midwives in the Bible. It is also full of humour, for instance when she narrates an anecdote about a woman whose husband complained that after giving birth her vagina was saggy, upon which she advised the woman ask her husband to check whether his manhood might have shrunk instead!

Poetry

Women were actively involved in writing and in publishing literature throughout this time. Isabella Whitney (*fl.* 1566–1573) was the first woman to write poetry for publication and to earn money. Although she was a gentlewoman, we know little about her as few records have survived about her life. Isabella's second and last work, a poetry collection called *A Sweet Nosegay, or Pleasant Posy*, appeared in 1573; in this work she maintained that since she was sound in mind and body but weak in purse, she had resolved to write to earn a living.

It is notable that America's first published poet was the English migrant Anne Bradstreet. Bradstreet is best known for her religious verse, but she also wrote poetry on topics as diverse as the reign of Queen Elizabeth I and the time her house burned down. Like many religious writers, Bradstreet saw the house fire as a lesson from God to remind her not to value material earthly possessions: 'The world no longer let me love; / My hope and treasure lies above.' Like the author of mothers' legacies, Anne wrote a poem to advise her husband in the event of her death in childbirth.

Her first book, *The Tenth Muse, Lately Sprung up in America*, was brought to England for publication in 1650 by her brother-in-law, and a corrected and expanded version was posthumously published in 1678, as *Several Poems Compiled with Great Variety of Wit*. This collection included the poem 'The Author to her Book' in which Anne makes the usual claims that her work was not good enough to have been published, calling it 'ill-formed offspring of my feeble brain,' and that it was published by well-meaning friends (her brother-in-law, in fact) who were 'less wise than true.'

However, later in the poem Anne remarks that if the authorship of the book might be queried, then the book should make it clear that it was written by her alone:

> *If for thy father asked, say, thou had none:*
> *And for thy mother she alas is poor,*
> *Which caused her thus to send thee out of door.*

The suggestion that people might assume the poetry was so good it was really written by a man reveals Anne's pride in it and her claim that it was only published for financial reasons belies her claim to have had it 'snatched' without her consent.

In the 1650s another woman, An Collins published her collection of poetry. All that is known about An exists within this book, as no further information about her has ever been found. *Divine Songs and Meditations* (1653) contains many poems in complicated verse forms, none of which are ever repeated within the volume. Her book is so rare that it only survives in a single copy, now preserved in an American library.

Collins' poetry implies that she suffered from ill health and was infertile, making her feel unlike other women, as she put it. Collins claimed to have been mocked by women for her amenorrhea and physical weakness, but she turned this quality into a positive trait within her poetry, claiming that childlessness gave her the space to be productive intellectually, instead of reproductively.

Prose Fiction

Novels as we know them today did not come into existence until the later seventeenth century, but prose fiction was already being published throughout the early modern era. Lady Mary Wroth (1587–1653) was the niece of the famous Renaissance poet Sir Philip Sidney and a courtier, known to have appeared in several court masques in the early 1600s. On the death of her husband in 1614, when she was left without any means of financial support, she turned to writing.

Her long pastoral prose romance *The Countess of Montgomery's Urania* (1621) was modelled on Sidney's *Arcadia*, but unlike the earlier text, it has a female hero. The book is a thinly-disguised fiction of the lives of some of the people at James I's court and on its publication caused a scandal, especially as it was written by a noblewoman; Wroth was shunned thereafter by her fellow courtiers. Appended to *Urania* was *Pamphilia to Amphilanthus* a sonnet sequence of over 80 poems, together with a number of other poems or 'songs.'

The heyday of the sonnet form had been in the late sixteenth century when her uncle wrote *Astrophil and Stella*, and Mary uses some of the conventions in Sidney's poems in her own sequence, the first written by a woman. Pamphilia's name means 'all-loving,' a name she lives up to, even dreaming of her lover as she praises sleep 'that gladly thee presents into my thought.' Much is made in the poems of Pamphilia's constancy to her lover, which has been viewed as a model of how the seventeenth century woman was supposed to behave. Yet, what is ground-breaking about the poems is that Pamphilia does not accept Amphilanthus' infidelity simply because it is a male trait, but instead wants him to change, ending the sequence with the appeal, 'now let your constancy your honour prove.'

Another noblewoman who published ground-breaking prose fiction in the seventeenth century, was Margaret Cavendish, Duchess of Newcastle, who published one of the first utopian novels, *The Description of a New World, Called the Blazing World* (1666). In this world, which comes to be ruled by the protagonist, a kidnapped maid, there is no war, and men and women are treated equally, spending their time in discussing philosophical questions together. Margaret was a prolific writer, publishing in many genres including a series of advisory letters to women (*Sociable Letters*, 1664) and a number of closet dramas, or plays, which were designed to be read rather than performed.

Other forms of fiction by women were emerging too with the works of professional playwright Aphra Behn (1640–1689). Her book, *Love Letters between a Nobleman and his Sister* ('sister,' in this context, means sister-in-law), published in three volumes between 1684 and 1687, was the very first epistolary novel to be published by a woman. Although Margaret Cavendish had published *Sociable Letters* in 1664, in which she wrote an agony-aunt style set of scenarios, Aphra Behn's work is different as it is an epistolary narrative developed through the letters. This style of fiction was to become very popular in the eighteenth century, with authors such as Samuel Richardson in his novels *Pamela* (1740), *Clarissa* (1747), and *Sir Charles Gradison* (1753).

Love Letters describes how Sylvia is seduced by her brother-in-law Philander and, like Mary Wroth's romance, Behn's novel draws on contemporary topics, for instance it contains veiled references to the Monmouth Rebellion (in which Charles II's illegitimate son James Scott, Duke of Monmouth, unsuccessfully tried to oust his Catholic uncle James II from the English throne). Aphra followed this up with the story of a slave, the eponymous *Oroonoko; or the Royal Slave* (1688), which is thought by some to be based on her own travels to Surinam, a Dutch African colony (now called the Republic of Suriname), in her youth.

In this tale Prince Oroonoko falls in love with Imoinda, whom the King wants to marry. At the end of the novella, Oroonoko suffers a gruesome death which he endures with dignity and 'thus died this great man; worthy of a better fate.' The novella tackles controversial topics, and includes scenes of violence and rape, but its prose form and its positive portrayal of a black character make it extremely innovative.

A number of short stories published in the 1690s are also thought to have been written by Aphra Behn. These stories which appeared in *The Histories and Novels of the Late Ingenious Mrs Behn*, contain examples of contemporary early modern medical thinking and folk cures. In 'The Unfortunate Bride; or The Blind Lady a Beauty,' Celesia's sight is restored by an itinerant witch-like healer, just as Lady Elizabeth Delaval described her toothache being cured in her 'Meditations.' Belvira tells her lover Frankwit that:

> *My poor Celesia now would charm your soul*
> *Her eyes, once blind, do now divinely roll.*
> *An aged matron has by charms unknown*
> *Given her clear sight as perfect as thy own.*

In another story, 'The Dumb Virgin,' Maria, the eponymous dumb virgin, suffers from an affliction which is described by Jane Sharp in her midwifery guide as a common one in young children. Maria is tongue-tied, a condition which does affect speech but does not necessarily lead to muteness. Nowadays the condition is thought to be a birth defect affecting 3-10 per cent of newborn babies.

In 'The Dumb Virgin' Maria's ankyloglossia is cured when she realises that she has been ruined by her own brother: 'Maria all this while had strong and wild convulsions of sorrow within her, till the working force of her anguish racking at once all the passages of her breast, by a violent impulse broke the ligament that doubled in her tongue.' After this, Maria, rather implausibly, is able to speak fluently and cry out that she has been incestuously seduced. The story, then, works as an inversion of the myth of Philomena, who was raped and mutillated by Tereus. This myth was well-known in early modern times, reworked by Shakespeare in *Titus Andronicus,* for example.

Public Plays and Closet Dramas

Plays were a prime form of early modern entertainment, especially for Londoners, many of whom attended the theatre on a regular basis. In Shakespeare's time you could buy a standing ticket to an outdoor performance at the Globe for a penny – the equivalent of about £5 today. As indoor theatres grew up, the price increased as the playhouses became more expensive to run, with highly priced candles needed to light the stage, for example, and the audience became more gentrified but it still remained a popular pastime.

The first play by a woman to be published was *The Tragedy of Mariam, the Fair Queen of Jewry*, which appeared in 1613. The play had been written around 10 years earlier by Lady Elizabeth Cary, Viscountess Falkland (1585–1639), designed to be read rather than performed. Elizabeth was a controversial figure, converting to Catholicism in 1626 and subsequently separating from her husband. This play is based on events in the life of the biblical figure King Herod and shows Mariam ruling her country jointly with her mother Alexandra after the tyrant, Herod's death.

In the royal courts of Elizabeth I and James I, masques were regularly staged and starred many prominent female courtiers, although a woman could not legitimately appear on the public stage until after the Restoration in 1660. All the key female roles associated with Shakespeare's plays, such as Juliet and Lady Macbeth, were played by boy actors before this time. During the Interregnum, however, the theatres were closed and public entertainment, such as bear baiting and cock-fighting, was banned. Puritan leaders saw theatres as hotbeds of sedition and corruption, and prominent Puritan William Prynne wrote that watching a play was likely to 'devirginate' an otherwise blameless young woman.

After the Restoration in 1660 Charles II immediately reopened the theatres, ordering that female roles should henceforth be played by women as he had become accustomed to seeing in France, claiming that this was less immoral than the practice of young men dressing up as women. This led to a number of women finding fame, fortune – and sometimes notoriety – on the London stage. Famous actresses of the time include Eleanor Gwyn, known as Nell, who began working as an orange seller to the theatre audiences, before becoming a famous actress and long-term mistress of the King.

The newly-reopened theatres also staged plays authored by women, and Aphra Behn is thought to be the first woman to have earned her living by playwriting. Between 1670–1687, Aphra wrote at least 17 plays, with a further two put on after her death. Playwriting was a precarious living, as payment depended upon the success of the play. The author received the takings from the third night's performance, so if the play failed to make a third night, then the author received no remuneration from it.

Aphra was a controversial playwright, whose Royalist political loyalties showed through in her works. *The Rover; or the Banished Cavaliers* (1677), for example, depicts impoverished cavaliers (soldiers on the Royalist side during the Civil Wars) displaced to Spain. Her plays often explore gender relations and show women's sexuality in ways that pushed contemporary boundaries, such as in the opening scene of *The Rover* in which two sisters Helena and Florinda discuss sex.

Florinda chides her sister for asking inappropriate questions, 'what an impertinent thing is a young girl bred in a nunnery? How full of questions?' leaving the audience in no doubt as to the nature of Helena's queries. Behn's plays also included uncomfortable scenes depicting sexual abuse of women; in *The Rover*, the cavaliers compare sword lengths to decide who is going to go first in attempted gang rape of Florinda.

Aphra suffered from accusations of plagiarism, for instance that *The Rover* drew heavily on Thomas Killigrew's *Thomaso* (1663). While there is no doubt that Aphra had based her play on Killigrew's, she defended her decision in the 'postscript' to the play: 'That I have stolen some hints from it [*Thomaso*], may be a proof that I valued it more than to pretend to alter it.' Playgoers, Aphra said, liked to show their 'breeding' by spotting allusions to other plays in the prologue to *Sir Patient Fancy* (1678), another of her plays, which was inspired by Moliere's *La Malade Imaginaire*, and such borrowing was standard practice in the Restoration.

Despite her prolific output, Aphra died in poverty. Yet, her plays are still read and performed today, and they are just as bawdy and outlandish as those by her male contemporaries. In particular, her plays often incorporate so-called 'breeched' roles, in which women dress in male clothing, adding titillation factor for the Restoration audience, who were able to glimpse the actresses' legs, then still rather a novelty.

Following Aphra's lead, Mary Pix (1666–1709) wrote at least a dozen plays for the Restoration stage from the 1690s; Catharine Trotter (c.1674-1749) had five plays performed; and Delarivier Manley (1663-1724), although now better known for her prose fiction *The New Atalantis* (1709), also had her plays staged throughout the 1690s.

Biography and Life Writing

One early female playwright, Lady Elizabeth Cary became the subject of a biography by her third daughter, Lucy Cary (1619–1650), which is predominantly a conversion narrative, encouraging readers to join the Catholic faith. Elizabeth herself wrote a fictionalised account of *The History of the Life, Reign, and Death of Edward II* around 1626, based closely on events at James I's court.

Having penned her autobiography, Margaret Cavendish published a biography of her husband William Cavendish, the Duke of Newcastle in 1667, *The Life of the Thrice Noble, High and Puissant Prince, William Cavendish, Duke, Marquis and Earl of Newcastle*. Diarist Samuel Pepys was famously unimpressed by it and recorded, on 18 March 1667, how he had spent an evening 'reading the ridiculous History of my Lord Newcastle, wrote by his wife, which shows her to be a mad, conceited, ridiculous woman, and he an ass to suffer her to write what she writes of to him, and of him.'

Women who transgressed the gender norms by writing for publication were subjected to censure at all levels of society. Pepys did not just dismiss the book, but he disparages it in terms of her gender rather than its literary merit, implying that Lord Newcastle should have known better than to allow his wife to publish it.

Early modern women were involved in all genres and forms of published and unpublished writing. For women of higher rank, writing was encouraged as a way of advising others, teaching and reflecting upon their lives. For other women, it was tricky to find the time. In order to write for publication, women did not only have to overcome the disparity in their education compared with that enjoyed by men, but also often had to balance work and childcare responsibilities. Sarah Jones whose book, *The Relation of a Gentlewoman long under the Persecution of the Bishops* which she self-published in 1642, records how she had to write at night by candlelight because of her household duties in the day, 'having not time in regard of my duties of my family.'

In addition to the types of writing discussed above, women published many religious conversion narratives, political tracts, and books of household management (which are covered in respective chapters within this book). As Virginia Woolf wrote in *A Room of One's Own* (1929), 'I would venture to guess that Anon, who wrote so many poems without signing them, was often a woman.' It is likely that far more anonymously published writing by the women of the seventeenth century still remains to be identified.

Bibliography

All early modern printed books were accessed via *Early English Books Online.*

Pre-1750 texts

Alleine, Theodosia, *Life and Death of the Rev. Joseph Alleine* (London, 1672)

Allen, Hannah, *A Narrative of God's Gracious Dealings with that Choice Christian Mrs Hannah Allen* (London: John Wallis, 1683)

[Anon.], *An Account of the Causes of Some Particular Rebellious Distempers viz. the Scurvy, Cancers in Women's Breasts, &c. Vapours, and Melancholy, &c. Weaknesses in Women* (London: [n. pub.], 1670)

[Anon.], *The London Jilt; or, The Politick Whore*, 2 vols (London, 1683)

[Anon.], *Aristotle's Master-Piece; or, The Secrets of Generation Display'd in all the Parts Thereof* (London: J. How, 1684)

[Anon.], *Mundus Muliebris: Or the Ladies Dressing-Room Unlocked and her Toilette Spread* (London: R. Bentley, 1690)

[Anon.], *Bloody News from Dover* (London, 1646)

[Anon.], *The Problems of Aristotle* (Edenborough, 1595)

[Anon.], *An Account of the Causes of some Particular Rebellious Distempers* (London: 1670)

[Anon.], *An Account of the General Nursery, or Colledg of Infants, set up by the Justices of Peace for the County of Middlesex* (London, 1686)

[Anon.], *The Women's Petition Against Coffee* (London, 1674)

[Anon.], *The Men's Answer to the Women's Petition Against Coffee, Vindicating Their own Performances* (London, 1674)

Astell, Mary, *A Serious Proposal to the Ladies* (London, 1694)

Austin, William, *Excellency of the Creation of Women* (London, 1658)

Bradstreet, Anne, *Several Poems compiled with Great Variety of Wit and Learning* (Boston MA, 1678)

Braithwaite, Richard, *Whimzies: Or, a New Cast of Characters* (London, 1631)

Bromfield, M., *A Brief Discovery of the Chief Causes, Signs, and Effects, of that most Reigning Disease, the Scurvy* (London, 1694)

Browne, Thomas, *Pseudodoxia Epidemica* (London: 1646)

Camden, William, *Remaines of a Greater Worke, concerning Britaine* (London, 1605)

Carleton, Mary, *The Case of Madam Mary Carleton* (London, 1663)

Cary, Elizabeth, *The Tragedy of Mariam, the Fair Queen of Jewry* (London, 1613)

Cavendish, Margaret, Countess of Newcastle, *The World's Olio* (London, 1655)

——, *Sociable Letters* (London, 1664)

——, *Observations upon Experimental Philosophy, to which is added. The Description of a New World called The Blazing World*. (London, 1666)

——, *The Life of the Thrice Noble, High and Puissant Prince, William Cavendish, Duke, Marquis and Earl of Newcastle* (London, 1667)

Chamberlayne, Edward, *The Present State of England* (London, 1669)

Chudleigh, Mary, *The Ladies Defence; Or, a Dialogue Between Sir John Brute, Sir William Loveall, Melissa, and a Parson* (London, 1701)

Clarke, Samuel, *England's Remembrancer* (London, 1677)

Cleaver, Robert and John Dod, *A Godly Form of Household Government for the Ordering of Private Families* (London, 1598)

Clinton, Elizabeth, *The Countess of Lincoln's Nursery* (Oxford, 1622)

Collins, An, *Divine Songs and Medications* (London, 1653)

Collier, Mary, *The Woman's Labour: an Epistle to Mr Stephen Duck* (London, 1739)

Croom, George, *The German Princess Revived; or The London Jilt* (London, 1683)

Crooke, Helkiah, *Mikrokosmographia: A Description of the Body of Man* (London, 1615)

Culpeper, Nicholas, *A Directory for Midwives; or, A Guide for Women, in their Conception, Bearing and Suckling their Children* (London, 1662)

Daffy, Anthony, *Daffy's Original and Famous Elixir Salutis: The Choice Drink of Health* (London, 1698)

Delaval, Lady Elizabeth, 'Meditations and Prayers,' Bodleian Library, Oxford, MS. Rawl. D. 78.

Dowe, Bartholomew, *A Dairy Book for Good Housewives* (London, 1588)

Drake, Judith, *An Essay in Defence of the Female Sex* (London, 1696)

Dufour, Philippe Sylvestre, *The Manner of Making of Coffee, Tea, and Chocolate* translated by John Chamberlayne (London, 1685)

Edgar, Thomas, *The Lawes Resolutions of Womens Rights* (London, 1632)

Evans, John, *John Evans, his Hummums is in Brownlow-Street in Drury-Lane* (London, 1679)

Featherstone Brown, Sarah and Thomas Brown, *Living Testimonies concerning the Death of the Righteous* (London, 1689)

Fiennes, Celia, *Through England on a Side Saddle in the time of William and Mary*, ed. by Mrs Griffiths (New York, 1888)

Freind, John, *Emmenologia*, trans. by Thomas Dale (London, 1729)

Gardiner, Ralph, *England's Grievance Discovered* (London, 1655)

Gerard, John, *The Herbal or General History of Plants* (London, 1633)

Gibson, Thomas, *The Anatomy of Humane Bodies Epitomised* (London, 1682)

Guillemeau, Jaques, *Childbirth; or, The Happy Delivery of Women* (London, 1612)

H. N., *The Ladies Dictionary, Being a General Entertainment of the Fair-Sex a Work Never Attempted Before in English* (London, 1694)

Harvey, Gideon, *The Conclave of Physicians* (London, 1686)

Herrick, Robert, *Hesperides; or, The Works Both Humane & Divine of Robert Herrick* (London, 1648)

Holinshed, Raphael, *The First and Second Volumes of Chronicles* (London, 1587)

Holme, Randle, *The Academy of Armory; or, A Storehouse of Armory and Blazon Containing the Several Variety of Created Beings* (Chester, 1688)

Jones, Sarah, *The Relation of a Gentlewoman long under the Persecution of the Bishops* (London: 1642)

Kent, Elizabeth Countess of, *A Choice Manual of Rare and Select Secrets in Physick and Surgery* (London, 1653)

Locke, John, *Some Thoughts Concerning Education* (London, 1693)

Langham, William, *The Garden of Health* (London, 1597)

Lanyer, Amelia, *Salve Deus Rex Judaeorum* (London, 1611)

Makin, Bathsua, *An Essay to Revive the Ancient Education of Gentlewomen* (London, 1673)

Markham, Gervase, *A Way to get Wealth, by Approved Rules of Practice in Good Husbandry and Housewifery* (London, 1625)

Marsh, A., *The Ten Pleasures of Marriage Relating All the Delights and Contentments that are Masked Under the Bands of Matrimony* (London, 1682)

Marten, John, *A Treatise of the Venereal Disease* (London, 1711)

Maubray, John, *The Female Physician Containing all the Diseases Incident to that Sex in Virgins, Wives and Widows* (London, 1724)

Oliver, John, *Present for Teeming Women, or, Scripture-directions for Women with Child how to Prepare for the Houre of Travel* (London, 1663)

Paré, Ambrose, *The Workes of That Famous Chirurgion Ambrose Parey*, trans. by T. Johnson (London, 1634)

Pechey, John, *The Compleat Midwife's Practice Enlarged* (London, 1698)

Piddlington, Rev., *A True Copy of the Paper Delivered the Night Before her Execution by Sarah Malcom* [sic.] *to the Rev. Mr. Piddington* (London, 1732)

Philips, Katherine, *Poems by the Most Deservedly Admired Mrs. Katherine Philips, the Matchless Orinda* (London, 1667)

Phillips, John, *Wit and Drollery Joviall Poems* (London, 1661)

Platter, Felix, *Golden Practice of Physick*, trans by Nicholas Culpeper (London, 1664)

Pliny the Elder, *The Historie of the World: Commonly Called, The Natural History of CPlinius Secundus*, trans. by Philemon Holland (London, 1634)

Porta, Giambattista della, *The Nineth Book of Natural Magic* (London, 1658 [orig. 1558])

Ray, John, *A collection of English Proverbs Digested into a Convenient Method for the Speedy Finding any one upon Occasion* (London, 1670)

Rivière, Lazare, *The Practice of Physick in Sixteen Several Books*, trans. by Nicholas Culpeper and others (London, 1655)

S.J., *Children's Diseases, Both Outward and Inward* (London, 1664)

Sennert, Daniel, *Practical Physick the Fourth Book in Three Parts*, trans N. Culpeper and Abdiah Cole (London, 1664)

Shelford, Robert, *Five Pious and Learned Discourses* (Cambridge, 1635)

Skelton, John, *Elynour Rummin, the Famous Ale-wife of England* (London, 1624)

Sowernam, Ester, *Ester Hath Hang'd Haman* (London, 1617)

Speght, Rachel, *A Mouzell for Melastomus* (London, 1617)

Sprint, John, *The Bride-Woman's Counsellor* (London, 1700)

Spooner, Thomas, *A Compendious Treatise of the Diseases of the Skin* (London: 1724)

Stone, Sarah, *A Complete Practice of Midwifery* (London, 1737)

Tryon, Thomas, *The Way to Save Wealth Shewing how a Man may Live Plentifully for Two-pence a Day* (London, 1695)

Tuke, Thomas, *A Discourse Against Painting and Tincturing of Women* (London, 1616)

W. T., *The Poet's Complaint: A Poem* (London, 1682)

Waller, Edmund, *The Second Part of Mr. Waller's Poems* (London, 1687)

Watkyns, Rowland, *Flamma Sine Fumo; or, Poems without Fictions* (London, 1662)

Wentworth, Anne, *A True Account of Anne Wentworth* (London,1676)

——, *England's Spiritual Pill* (London, 1679)

Whately, William, *A Bride-Bush; or, A Wedding Sermon* (London, 1617)

Whitney, Isabella, *A Sweet Nosegay, or Pleasant Posy* (London, 1573)

Woolley, Hannah, *The Accomplished Lady's Delight* (London, 1675)

——, *The Complete Servant-maid; or, the Young Maiden's Tutor* (London, 1677)

Wroth, Lady Mary, *The Countess of Montgomery's Urania* (London, 1621)

[Venette, Nicolas de], *The Mysteries of Conjugal Love Reveal'd* (London, 1707)

Post 1750 texts

Adcock, Rachel, Sara Read, and Anna Ziomek, eds., *Flesh and Spirit: An Anthology of Seventeenth century Women's Writing* (Manchester: MUP, 2014)

Anger, Jane, 'Jane Anger, her Protection for Women,' in *Women's Writing of the Early-Modern Period, 1588-1688: An Anthology*, ed. by Stephanie Hodgson-Wright (Edinburgh: Edinburgh University Press, 2002)

Aughterson, Kate, *Renaissance Women: A Sourcebook: Constructions of Femininity in England* (London: Routledge, 1995)

Beer, Anna, *Bess: The Life of Lady Ralegh, Wife to Sir Walter* (London: Constable and Richardson, 2005)

Bickerton Williams, John, *Memoirs of the Life and Character of Mrs. Sarah Savage to which are added Memoirs of her Sister, Mrs Hulton* (London: Holdsworth and Ball, 1829)

Bradstreet, Anne, *The Works of Anne Bradstreet in Prose and Poetry*, ed. by John Harvard Ellis (Gloucester: Peter Smith, 1962)

Brown, Silvia, ed., *Women's Writing in Stuart England: The Mothers' Legacies of Dorothy Leigh, Elizabeth Joscelin and Elizabeth Richardson* (Stroud: Sutton, 1999)

Brydges, Cassandra, *Cassandra Brydges (1670-1735) First Duchess of Chandos: Life and Letters*, ed by Rosemary O'Day (Woodbridge: Boydell Press, 2007)

Bunyan, John, *Grace Abounding with Other Spiritual Autobiographies*, ed by John Stachniewski and Anita Pacheco (Oxford: Oxford World's Classics, 1998)

Camden, Vera J., ed., *The Narrative of the Persecutions of Agnes Beaumont* (Michigan, IL: Colleagues Press, 1992)

Clark, Alice, *Working Life of Women in the Seventeen Century* (London: Routledge, 1919)

Clifford, Arthur, ed., *Tixall Poetry* (Edinburgh: James Ballantyne, 1813)

Clifford, Lady Anne, *The Diaries of Lady Anne Clifford*, ed. by D. J. H. Clifford (Stroud: Sutton, 1992)

Cockayne, Emily, *Hubbub: Filth, Noise and Stench in England* 1600–1770 (New Haven: Yale University Press, 2007)

Cook, Judith, *Dr Simon Forman: A Most Notorious Physician* (London: Vintage, 2001)

Crawford, Patricia, *Blood, Bodies and Families in Early Modern England* (Harlow: Pearson, 2004)

——, *Women and Religion in England, 1500–1720* (London: Routledge, 1993)

—— and Laura Gowing, *Women's Worlds in Seventeenth-Century England 1580–1720: A Source Book* (London: Routledge, 1999)

Cressy, David, *Birth, Marriage, and Death: Ritual, Religion, and the Life-Cycle in Tudor and Stuart England* (Oxford: Oxford University Press, 1997)

Defoe, Daniel, *The Complete English Gentleman* (London: Ballantyne, Hanson and Co., 1890)

Delaval, Lady Elizabeth, *The Meditations of Lady Elizabeth Delaval*, ed by Douglas D. Green (Gateshead: Northumberland Press, 1978)

Eales, Jacqueline, *Women in Early Modern England 1500–1700* (London: University College London Press, 1998)

Evelyn, John, *The Diary of John Evelyn*, ed. by E. S. De Beer (London: Oxford University Press, 1959)

Fildes, Valerie, *Breasts, Bottles and Babies: A History of Infant Feeding* (Edinburgh: Edinburgh University Press, 1986)

——, *Wet Nursing: A History from Antiquity to the Present* (Oxford: Blackwell, 1988)

Fissell, Mary E., *Vernacular Bodies: The Politics of Reproduction in Early Modern England* (Oxford: Oxford University Press, 2004)

Fox, Louisa Lane, *Love to the Little Ones: The Trials and Triumphs of Parents Throughout the Ages* (London: Francis Lincoln, 2009)

Foxcroft, Louise, *Calories and Corsets: A History of Dieting over 2,000 Years* (London: Profile, 2011)

Fraser, Antonia, *The Weaker Vessel: Woman's Lot in Seventeenth-Century England* (London: Phoenix Press, 1984)

Froide, Amy M., *Never Married: Single Women in Early Modern England* (Oxford: Oxford University Press, 2007)

Gowing, Laura, *Common Bodies: Women, Touch and Power in Seventeenth-Century England* (London: Yale University Press, 2003)

Graham, Elspeth, Hilary Hinds, Elaine Hobby and Helen Wilcox, *Her Own Life: Autobiographical Writings by Seventeenth century English Women* (London: Routledge, 1989)

Greer, Germaine, Jeslyn Medoff, Melinda Sansone, and Susan Hastings, eds, *Kissing the Rod: An Anthology of 17th Century Women's Verse* (London: Virago, 1988)

Hagar, Alan, *Encyclopedia of British Writers, 16th, 17th, and 18th Centuries* (New York: Bookbuilders, 2005)

Harley, Brilliana, Lady, *Letters of the Lady Brilliana Harley, Wife of Sir Robert Harley, of Brampton Bryan, Knight of the Bath*, ed. by Thomas Taylor Lewis (London: Camden Society, 1854)

Heighes Woodforde, Dorothy, ed., *Woodforde Papers and Diaries* (London: Peter Davies, 1932)

Hobby, Elaine, *Virtue of Necessity, English Women's Writing 1649-88* (Ann Arbor: University of Michigan Press, 1989)

Hodgkin, Katharine, *Women, Madness and Sin in Early Modern England: The Autobiographical Writings of Dionys Fitzherbert* (Farnham: Ashgate, 2010)

Houlbooke, Ralph, *Death, Religion, and the Family in England, 1480-1750* (Oxford: Oxford University Press, 2000)

——, ed., *English Family Life, 1576–1716: An Anthology from Diaries* (Oxford: Basil Blackwell, 1988)

Hughes, Talbot, *Dress Design: An Account for Artists and Dressmakers* (ebook: Project Gutenberg, 2011)

Hutchinson, Lucy, *A Memoir of the Life of Colonel Hutchinson*, ed. by Julius Hutchinson (London, 1806)

Josselin, Ralph *The Diary of Ralph Josselin*, ed. by Alan MacFarlane (Oxford: Oxford University Press, 1991)

Thomas Knyvett, *The Knyvett Letters (1620-1644)*, ed. by Bertram Schofield (London: Constable and Company, 1949)

Lane, Joan, ed., *John Hall and his Patients: The Medical Practice of Shakespeare's Son-in-Law* (Stratford: The Birthplace Trust, 1996)

Laurence, Anne, *Women in England 1500-1700: A Social History* (London: Weidenfeld and Nicolson, 1995)

Loftis, John, ed., *The Memoirs of Anne, Lady Halkett and Ann, Lady Fanshawe* (Oxford: Clarendon Press, 1979)

Matthews, Sara F. Grieco, 'Breastfeeding, Wet Nursing and Infant Mortality in Europe (1400-1800),' in *Historical Perspectives on Breastfeeding: Two Essays by Sara F. Matthews and Carlo A. Corsini* (Unicef, 1991) <www.unicef.irc.org/publications/pdf>

Moody, Joanna, ed., *The Private Life of an Elizabethan Lady: The Diary of Lady Margaret Hoby, 1599-1605* (Stroud: Sutton, 2001)

Moore, Rosemary, *Light in Their Consciences: The Early Quakers in Britain, 1646-1666* (Pennsylvania: Penn State University Press, 2000)

Mordaunt, Elizabeth Viscountess, *The Private Diarie*, ed. by Earl of Rodin (Duncairn: 1856)

Pennington, Mary, *Experiences in the Life of Mary Pennington (Written by Herself)*, ed. by Norman Penney (London: Healey, 1911)

Picard, Liza, *Restoration London* (London: Phoenix Press, 1997)

Pollock, Linda, *With Faith and Physic: The Life of a Tudor Gentlewoman Lady Grace Mildmay, 1552–1620* (New York: Collins and Brown, 1993)

Raynalde, Thomas, *The Birth of Mankind: Otherwise Named, The Woman's Book*, ed. by Elaine Hobby (Aldershot: Ashgate, 2009)

Read, Sara, *Menstruation and the Female Body in Early Modern England* (Basingstoke: Palgrave Macmillan, 2013)

Rich, Mary, Countess of Warwick, *The Autobiography of Mary Countess of Warwick*, ed. by Thomas Crofton Crocker (London: Percy Society, 1848; Kessinger facsimile reprint, 2009)

Schofield, Bertram, *The Knyvett Letters (1620–1644)* (London: Constable, 1649)

Searle, Arthur, ed., *Barrington Family Letters: 1628–1632* (London: Royal Historical Society, 1983)

Sharp, Jane, *The Midwives Book; or, The Whole Art of Midwifry Discovered*, ed. by Elaine Hobby (New York and Oxford: Oxford University Press, 1999)

Smith, Virginia, *Clean: A History of Personal Hygiene and Purity* (Oxford: Oxford University Press, 2007)

Steele, Valerie, *The Corset: A Cultural History* (New York, NY: Yale University Press, 2003)

Storey, M. J., ed. *Two East Anglian Diaries 1641-1729: Isaac Archer and William Coe* (Woodbridge: Boydell, 1994)

Teonge, Henry, *The Diary of Henry Teonge, Chaplain on Board His Majesty's Ships Assistance, Bristol, and Royal Oak, Anno 1675 to 1679*, ed by Charles Knight (London, 1825)

Thompson, E. M., ed. *Correspondence of the Family of Hatton, Chiefly Letters Addressed to Christopher First Viscount Hatton, A. D. 1601-1704* (London: Camden Soc., 1878-9)

Thornton, Alice, *The Autobiography of Alice Thornton*, ed. by Charles Jackson (London: Mitchell and Hughes, 1875)

Vincent, Susan J., *The Anatomy of Fashion: Dressing the Body from the Renaissance to Today* (Berg, 2009)

Wall, Alison D., *Two Elizabethan Women: Correspondence of Joan and Maria Thynne* (Devises: Wiltshire Record Society, 1983)

Whitaker, Kate, *Mad Madge: Margaret Cavendish, Duchess of Newcastle, Royalist, Writer and Romantic* (London: Chatto and Windus, 2003)

Williams, John Bickerton, *Memoirs of the Life and Character of Mrs. Sarah Savage to which are added Memoirs of her Sister, Mrs Hulton* (London: Holdsworth and Ball, 1829)

Wilmot, John, Earl of Rochester, *Selected Works*, ed. by Frank H. Ellis (London: Penguin, 1994)

Yalom, Marilyn, *A History of the Breast* (New York, NY: Ballantine, 1997)

——, *A History of the Wife* (New York: Harper Collins, 2001)

Websites

The Worshipful Company of Bakers www.bakers.co.uk

The Records of the Old Bailey, 1674-1913 www.oldbaileyonline.org

Early Modern Medical articles www.earlymodernmedicine.com

The British Civil War Project http://bcw-project.org

The Oxford Dictionary of National Biography www.oxfordnb.com

The Diary of Samuel Pepys www.pepysdiary.com

My Tudor Court www.tudorplace.com.ar

'Women Printers and Booksellers of the 17th Century' http://library.missouri.edu

Index

Where dates of birth and death are known, they are given in the index.